Academic
SLIDE DESIGN

Academic
SLIDE DESIGN

Visual Communication
for Teaching and Learning

ANN FANDREY

SCALE&FINE

Cover art: IFC Design
Cover design: Laura Drew
Page design: Trio Bookworks

Publishing Consultant: Ann Delgehausen, Trio Bookworks

Library of Congress Control Number: 2017905046

ISBN, print: 978-0-9988682-0-2
ISBN, ebook: 978-0-9988682-1-9

Printed in the United States of America
21 20 19 18 17   1 2 3 4 5 6 7 8 9 10

Contents

Introduction   1

Lessons for Designing
Engaging, Effective Slides

1   Beautiful, Functional Designs   9
2   Multimedia Learning and Design   17
3   Accessible, Functional Slide Decks   25
4   Accessible, Functional Handouts   33
5   Unbulleting 1: Visual Designs That Aren't Bullets   41
6   The Power of White Space   53
7   Unbulleting 2: The Assertion-Evidence Structure   59
8   Selecting Illuminative Visuals   69
9   Unbulleting 3: Communicating Meaning
     through Spatial Positioning   81
10   Layout and Composition   93
11   Effective Use of Color for Teaching and Learning   107
12   Effective Typography for Teaching and Learning   123
13   Techniques for Guiding Attention   145
14   Bullet Point Master Class   155
15   Good Digital Citizenry   167
16   The Academic Slide Design Method   179

Principles of Academic Slide Design   187
Further Reading   191
Works Consulted   193
Figure and Source Credits   203
Index   209

Introduction

Welcome to *Academic Slide Design: Visual Communication for Teaching and Learning*. This book combines what is known about multimedia learning, universal design, visual perception, and graphic design to create a new vision and new method for building more effective slides. The goal of this book is to teach you—the busy educator or instructional designer—how to apply techniques of effective visual communication toward creating slides that better assist students with understanding and remembering information conveyed during live lectures.

Several decades of research in multimedia learning design have shown that slides full of bullet points are ineffective for helping students understand and remember content delivered during live lectures. While people who study this sort of thing have now realized that text-heavy slides aren't effective, most of us still can't seem to break the habit. When we try to buck the convention of the traditional topic-subtopic slide design by adding more graphics, we accidentally run the other direction toward decorative designs that obscure the important points we need to make.

This book will help you learn to think more graphically and less textually in creating slides for teaching and learning. I hope it also will inspire you to think more globally about the accessibility and functionality of your slides and slide decks.

Unlike other books that take a topics-based approach to teaching slide design, this book is organized in a lesson format. I explain why certain styles and habits are ineffective, and how you can do better. Most importantly, I'll show you lots of examples of more effective designs. These sixteen lessons, complete with learning objectives and exercises for you to complete on your own, will reinvigorate your slide design practice.

Reading This Book for Some Quick Fixes

If you just want to improve the way your existing slides look, read these lessons:

Lesson 6   **The Power of White Space**
Lesson 8   **Selecting Illuminative Visuals**
Lesson 11   **Effective Use of Color for Teaching and Learning**
Lesson 12   **Effective Typography for Teaching and Learning**
Lesson 14   **Bullet Point Master Class**

You may also want to skip to the end and read the Principles of Academic Slide Design section, which presents the main ideas in a checklist format.

Reading This Book for the Big Picture

However, if you're here to transform the way you design slides, you'll want to read the whole book. The lessons are sequenced to help you develop visual communication competencies, though you may decide to create your own path through the material. Begin with this list, which is an overview of the key arguments.

1. Writing is thinking, and slide design is visual writing. Learning to make better slides will make you a better visual designer and a better lecturer, because you'll be forced to become more intentional and more precise.

2. Slide design starts with the lecture's content and structure rather than with the slides. Don't open PowerPoint right away. Doing so will result in a slide deck that privileges the slides over the content rather than the other way around. You need to script and plan first.

3. When you use visuals to accompany a lecture, they become a part of the experience of your lecture. Just as you strive to write clear, consistent, cohesive lectures, so too should you analogously strive to create clear, consistent, cohesive visual aids. The lecture is a holistic experience of visual and verbal information.

4. Pretty slides don't work better simply because they're pretty; they work better because the attributes that make them pretty also make them more functional. Some attributes that contribute to prettyness are clarity, consistency, and cohesion.

5. Consistent design decisions on each slide make for cohesive slide decks overall.

6. Decide on a consistent color system, perhaps four colors, and stick with it throughout the deck. The colors should contrast well when displayed against each other and against the slide background.

7. Select a consistent font and stick with it throughout the deck. The font should be plain rather than decorative.

8. Every element that appears on the slide canvas contributes to students' experience because they will immediately attempt either to read it or otherwise ascribe meaning to everything in the display. Learn to articulate the reasons for each of your design decisions. You should have a reason for every slide and a reason for everything on the slide.

9. People can't read and listen at the same time. Key to most (mis)uses of bullet points is that they create text-heavy slides. Text-heavy slide designs force students to divide their attention between reading your slides and listening to you. Put fewer words on each slide.

10. Students tend to prioritize the information on the slides over the words you're actually saying. You become a sidekick to your slides rather than the other way around.

11. To restore an appropriate relationship between you and your slides and to relieve your slides of so many words, learn to think more visually and less textually. Identify those parts of your content that lend themselves to a visual treatment.

12. Images, charts, graphs, and video clips are obvious visual solutions, but you also can communicate information via shapes and lines that show relationships. The composition of the slide also communicates meaning.

13. Selection of graphics is key. Visuals on slides should be used as a means to illuminate concepts and reinforce main ideas rather than replicate or simply illustrate your messages.

14. Think function over decoration when designing slides. Those graphics and pictures you put on slides to jazz them up shouldn't be on there just to add visual interest.

15. Another way to offload text-heavy material—which doesn't belong on slides—is to turn it into a handout you prepare in a word processing application and distribute separately to students.

16. Some of your slides should function as organizational supports: preview slides to give an overview of the material, guidepost slides to remind your audience (and you) where they are in the lecture, and recap slides to review and reinforce main ideas.

17. Consider white space your best tool for providing breathing room on the slide and for showing emphasis of important material. White space works better than annotations, underlines, boldface type, exclamation marks, or any other static means of highlighting important material.

18. The effectiveness of visuals is part how they look and part how you interact with them. Progressive disclosure and signaling techniques, accomplished using the presentation software's animation feature, can help guide students' attention during your talks.

19. Not every point you make needs to be on a slide. Sometimes a message is communicated best verbally rather than visually.

You're no doubt planning your next lecture right now. Let's get started!

Lessons for Designing Engaging, Effective Slides

Beautiful, Functional Designs

It's widely accepted that beautiful things work better, but why is this true?*
In the pages that follow, you'll learn there is a direct relationship between slide
designs that are pretty and ones that are functional. You'll start to develop an
awareness of and basic vocabulary for the qualities that make it so. In this first
lesson, we'll analyze exactly what you're responding to when you see a beautiful
graphic design so that you can evaluate your own slide designs and decide how to
improve them. As your awareness of what makes a design effective and functional
grows, so too will your ability to create more effective, functional slides.

The Functional Role of Pretty Things

For nearly a decade I provided instructional design support to busy
physicians who practiced and taught at a university hospital. I worked
on slide decks of fifty, sixty, eighty slides that were crammed to the
margins with textbook facts delineated by bullets.

Teaching physicians often asked me to take slides like these and
"make them pretty" the week before (or the day before) a lecture or
conference presentation. So I did what I could with them: I made sure
the font was the same throughout the deck, that the bullet points
followed a logical hierarchy, that acronyms were spelled out, and that

---

* This idea is from the influential essay "Emotion and Design: Attractive Things Work
 Better" by Donald A. Norman.

typos were corrected. I removed decoration. I aligned and balanced the composition of the slides to make space around important information. I loved this work. It was completely satisfying, and I felt useful. But the word *pretty* in that context really started to get my goat after a while.

Why? Because I realized that what I was really doing for these decks was to make them more effective as teaching materials.

This "prettying up" actually served to make the meaning clearer and more apprehensible so students and audiences in conference ballrooms, clinic workrooms, and lecture halls could focus on the message of the talk. They wouldn't have to strain to read or make sense of what was often a convoluted or completely unorganized slide.

The word *pretty* unintentionally trivializes the important work that is design. People often tend to think of prettyness as a cosmetic quality: surface level and a nice addition, but certainly not essential. Now is the time to give proper credit to the impact pretty has on the visual display of information. Consider these points about the difference prettyness makes.

1. Pretty plays an essential role in information clarity. Students can't acquire knowledge if the information isn't clear in the first place.

2. Pretty plays a functional role in gaining students' attention. Students won't learn when they're not motivated to try and make sense of an overwhelming slide, or if they can't find a point of entry into a slide that is a wall of words.

3. Pretty plays a functional role in maintenance of attention over time. In the absence of within-slides consistency and across-slides cohesion, students may eventually give up trying to figure out what you and your slides are trying to say.

4. Pretty also plays a supportive role in understanding and remembering. Simply, if students didn't notice or didn't pay attention to the message in the first place, how can they remember it later, let alone apply it in new situations?

5. Not to mention, pretty contributes to the creation of unified, cohesive-looking slide decks, which can affect your professional credibility.

To be fair and precise, I wasn't "designing" back in the day, at least not in the structural sense. But the cosmetic and structural also have an intricate relationship: design is serious work that requires training, apprenticeship, practice, and commitment. Designers spend years learning not only how to create effective designs but also how to discuss and defend those decisions. The decisions that designers make are always toward the functional and intentional rather than the random, haphazard, or purely decorative.

I hope that you'll cease to dismiss the value of visually attractive slides as simply pretty and start thinking in terms of functionality. Prettyness is intricately connected with your slides' function as effective visual aids. Functional slides clearly communicate the intended message.

Attributes of Prettyness

What are the surface-level qualities that people are responding to when they say your slides are pretty? Let's explore this question in terms of three "ugly" slides and their "pretty" makeovers. Then we'll identify some key characteristics that contribute to prettyness. Remember, pretty equals functional, so the real question is: What qualities make a design more functional?

Consider the slide depicted in Figure 1.1. You've seen this type of slide before, a design I'll refer to throughout the book as the topic-subtopic structure (terminology that is borrowed from the work of

1.1

Joanna Garner, Michael Alley and colleagues). You might even have spent a moment wondering what is wrong with it. What words would you use to describe it? Perhaps *busy, complex, crowded*, and *cluttered* come to mind. Compare it with its makeover (Figure 1.2). Words you might use to describe this slide are clear, focused, simple, and spacious. The makeover also happens to look so drastically different that you might not even believe it deals in the same subject matter as the original.

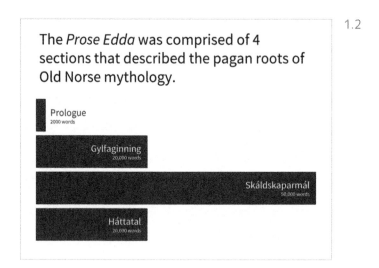

1.2

In a second set of slides, you could describe the ugly original (Figure 1.3) as mismatched, wordy, and unbalanced. It's impossible to tell at a glance what the slide is about, and you don't necessarily want to spend a lot of time figuring it out because the color scheme and styling of the background make it appear dated. The makeover (Figure 1.4) is more visually appealing because it stands to prove just one point as simply as possible.

The ugly slide in Figure 1.5 is cluttered and disjointed. The data table is too small to read, and it's so low resolution that it appears a bit fuzzy. The column of survey design information is hard to read because the differing amounts of space between words are distracting. The photograph at the bottom left looks like it was added as an after-thought. Last, the slide seems to be presenting at least three different topics. By contrast, the makeover (Figure 1.6) is, once again, focused and clear. It presents one main idea and gives that idea plenty of breathing room.

1.3

Buffer strips

- Area of land maintained in permanent vegetation that helps to control air, soil, and water quality, other environmental problems
- Primarily on agricultural land
- Trap sediment, and enhance filtration of nutrients and pesticides by slowing down runoff that could enter the local surface waters
- Root systems of the planted vegetation in these buffers hold soil particles together - alleviate soil of wind erosion and stabilize stream banks providing protection against substantial erosion, landslides
- Can also improve farming safety and efficiency
- Types: grassed waterway, contour buffer strips, vegetative barriers, field borders, filter strips, riprap

1.4

Buffer strips improve soil, water, and air quality.

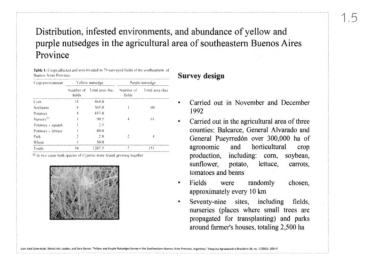

1.5

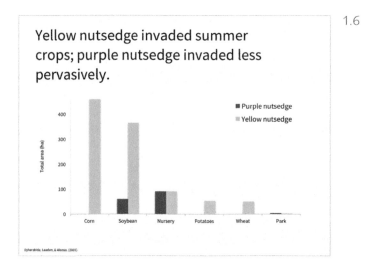

1.6

In all three of these comparisons, notice how the lists of descriptors we've gathered contain a mix of attributes of information (complex, focused, simple) alongside attributes normally used for visual presentation (crowded, cluttered, spacious). The presentation—that is, the visual experience of a design—is closely tied to your perception of the quality of the information contained in it.

What makes the original versions so uninviting to look at, while their makeovers are so much more appealing? Consider the words that surfaced as each set was discussed. Pleasing designs communicate a single message, so they are focused rather than overwhelming or digressive. They are precise rather than ambiguous, confounding, or confusing. Their messages are easily apprehensible because they're spacious rather than crowded, cramped, or cluttered; their designs balance space with the other elements on the slide. They are orderly rather than erratic or haphazard. Each of these attributes (focused, precise, spacious, and orderly) leads to a condition of information clarity.

Those characteristics that you thought were subjective, surface-level impressions (the features and aspects you were responding to when you tried to determine what was pretty and ugly) are actually intimately tied to whether the slide effectively communicates the intended message. Prettyness clearly isn't just about surface characteristics.

Intentionality Begets Better Designs

Clear communication is always the result of intentional—rather than arbitrary—design decisions. Always start with this goal: not just, What is this slide trying to say? but rather, What am I trying to say that I need a visual aid to help me show or to help back me up?

Slides also are rarely seen in nature just by themselves; they travel in packs. Consider the cohesion of the slides together as part of the deck. You achieve cohesion across a deck by adhering to a consistent set of design decisions from slide to slide. A cohesive deck is important because the slides are visual aids to the lecture, and the lecture overall needs to be cohesive. Throughout your own lecture planning process, you can repeat these three words to yourself:

clear   consistent   cohesive

They create an alliterative little mantra that can help remind you of the keys to successful visual communication. And you can leverage these qualities to create more effective designs.

EXERCISES

1. Look around. This week, look around you and begin to notice the graphic designs that catch your eye: professionally designed posters, billboards, and newspaper and magazine ads. What elements of the design caught your attention? How would you describe your reactions to any of these designs? What words would you ascribe: *beautiful, bland, spare, complex, balanced*? Try and articulate as specifically as possible what aspects of the design please or displease you. Capture your first impressions; you're just starting out here, and you're just starting to hone your awareness of the designs all around you. You can learn a lot about design just by taking notice of what makes a professional designer's work effective. Just as instructive, notice ways an inexperienced designer's work is less effective.

2. Start a visual journal. A natural extension of the exercise above is to begin to keep a visual journal, as design students and professional designers do. In a visual journal you collect examples of designs and your reflections on them. In developing this perhaps lifelong habit, the more you look, the more you see, and the stronger your visually literate eye will become.

Multimedia Learning and Design

The biggest problem with the topic-subtopic slide structure is that if you're doing it this way, you're probably trying to do three things at once. You're using a medium that was intended for the creation of visual aids to do triple duty in creating visual aids, speaker notes, and handouts. It just doesn't work. Like most things that attempt to fulfill several disparate functions at the same time, you end up doing none of them well. It's the same with slides.   In this lesson, we'll look closely at the history of the traditional topic-subtopic slide structure: its rise to power, its proven lack of fitness for rule, and why you should elect a different design to govern your slide canvases. Then we'll review the basic principles of multimedia learning theory and examine ways these principles can help you structure your slides more effectively. By the end of this chapter, I hope you'll be inspired to learn some new methods.

Slides Should Be Slides (Not Speaker Notes or Handouts)

Over the past thirty years, public speaking professionals—teachers, salespeople, evangelizers, and other experts—have taken a graphical software designed to help users create visual aids for presentations and followed its design prompts (as depicted in Figure 2.1) a little too closely.

The software commanded: "Click to add text," and text we did add! The software conveniently, automatically formatted that text as bullet

2.1

points. The bullets felt familiar, much like the outline of a research paper, another type of academic writing. A consequence of following the design prompts: our presentations and lectures came to consist almost entirely of lists of facts.

We then took these slides with us when we spoke in front of groups of people. We realized that we could use them like a teleprompter, which helped us remember what we wanted to say. When our time ran out, no matter; our audiences could still access the rest of what we'd planned to say because we'd used the Print > Handout button and had brought along stapled photocopies of the slides, three per page with lines for manual note taking.

In short, we adopted a habit of trying to use slides as visual aids, teleprompter, and handouts all at once, and this ineffective, pervasive habit has had consequences.

Using slides as speaker notes or a teleprompter creates problems for both speaker and audience. Speakers who simply read their slides out loud are much less dynamic; they're likely not connecting with the audience. When slides have too many words on them, viewers tend to read ahead instead of listening, which happens in boardrooms as often as classrooms. Students can't listen to you while they're reading the content on the slide. Slides full of information require students to split their attention between two separate messaging streams and force them to choose where they'll direct their attention. Under these conditions, students might successfully attend to one or the other, or they might panic and miss everything.

We need a better way.

We need to reposition slides as a tool that helps us do one thing: teach more effectively during lecture. I'm suggesting that you create visual aids, speaking notes, and a separate handout for your students' consumption. Three different contexts, three different instructional resources. Does this sound insane? It's far from insane, it's necessary, and it's long overdue; the traditional topic-subtopic slide design will never be effective as long as human cognitive architectures are as they are.

How Multimedia Learning Works

Richard Mayer, the most well-known, prolific, and oft-cited researcher in the field of multimedia learning, explains that multimedia learning theory is founded on three coordinating theories. First, dual channel theory states that our brains have separate channels for processing verbal and visual material. Second, we have limited capacity for processing incoming information; we can only process small amounts of information at one time. Third, the theory of active processing suggests that we need to engage in appropriate cognitive processing of new information in order to integrate it with what we already know. Appropriate cognitive processing is

1. noticing and paying attention to incoming information;

2. organizing it into meaningful mental representations, which can be either verbal or pictorial representations; and

3. connecting these verbal and pictorial representations with information that we understand already.*

> * This is Richard Mayer's selection, organization, and integration (SOI) model of meaningful learning, as described in "Learning Strategies for Making Sense out of Expository Text."

Words and pictures come into our brains through sensory channels—what we see and what we hear. We process new information in working memory, and we transfer the information to long-term memory.

In a live lecture, information coming in via sensory inputs is transient: your students are watching and listening to you in real time without benefit of pause, replay, or closed-captioning controls. Thoughtfully designed presentations support learning in these circumstances by

• organizing the content around one central idea;

- providing evidence in support of the central idea;

- showing students the organizational structure of the talk;

- reminding students periodically where they are in the context of this content; and

- showing visuals (slides) that have been designed to integrate—rather than compete—with incoming verbal information.

Visuals compete with verbal information when there are too many words on the slide and the words are the same or similar to what's being spoken. This is the principle of redundancy, well researched and almost unanimously conclusive that seeing written words interferes with the comprehension of simultaneously spoken words.

Visuals compete with verbal information when there are decorative pictures on the slide. Though pictures are processed by a different and more automatic part of the brain than verbal information, their presence still increases the amount of processing the student has to do to figure out whether the pictures are relevant or not.

Visuals compete with verbal information when the display is disorganized or unnecessarily complex and offers no clear point of entry to the design. Any amount of time the student spends struggling to figure out how to learn from the slide is time wasted in conflict with what the instructor is saying.

By contrast, visuals integrate with verbal information when the content of the slide complements what's being said, when students can instantly apprehend the message of the slide, and when the instructor can use the slide to show why the information is true.

It's virtually impossible for slides to serve a triple function as visual aids, speaker notes, and handout if they are to integrate, rather than compete, with the verbal portion of your lecture. Let's agree moving forward that the role of slides—if you are to follow the academic slide design method—is as visual aids to your verbally delivered lectures.

Do You Need a Slide at All?

Slides are meant to be visual *aids*. The purpose of visual aids in a talk is not to provide students with a text-based version of what you're saying out loud, but rather to illuminate and enhance your talk. You don't need a slide for everything in your presentation. Sometimes the best way to help students focus their attention is to provide a blank backdrop so they can focus on the story you're telling. How to determine whether you need a slide or not?

A slide is warranted when it

- provides a visual means of organization for forthcoming information (a preview slide);

- helps students locate where they are in the lecture (a guidepost slide);

- shows a concept, process, relationship, or idea via a graph, chart, diagram, image, or other visuospatial treatment;

- maps directly to the learning objectives or outcomes of your talk—that is, you're showing something that really does deserve to be powerfully pointed at; or

- contributes to a climate of good digital citizenry (e.g., source citations and references).

A good guideline to keep in mind: You *should* make a slide anytime you want to show—rather than just tell—your audience something.

Slides aren't meant to substitute for what you plan to say or to help you remember what you want to say. You might not need a slide in these situations:

- You find yourself writing nonessential facts or statistics on a slide so you don't forget to mention them. Anything you wouldn't expect students to be able to recite from memory likely doesn't need to be on a slide.

- Try as you might, you can't figure out an effective design. If your design ideas feel contrived or gimmicky, or if on testing it with a group of students you see that the design confuses rather than clarifies the idea, it's a sign you may not need a slide.

- You realize that the design is entirely ornamental, without even an affective function, such as giving students some type of mental break after a section of complex material.

As you develop your visual literacy skills, challenge yourself to become as intentional as possible with each of your design decisions. You should be able to articulate the functional reason for each element on the slide and for each slide in the deck. If you can't, or if the designs you've come up with simply aren't successful (based on student feedback), then you're likely better off deleting them so students can do some extra-deep listening.

Unimodal Slide Designs

This book provides design guidelines for presentations that are primarily multimodal, that is, where the slides accompany verbally delivered presentations, which is the traditional use of presentation software.

However, technology now enables us to design and display presentations right in the cloud, and further, to publish and embed our slide decks in web pages, using iframes. Instructional materials are evolving based on these new affordances, which leverage presentation software's ease of use for controlling layout and typography without needing to know any HTML or CSS.

Educators are now producing slide decks that can be consumed in a single modality, referred to as *unimodal*—a personal reading experience without a separate verbal track. It's important to be able to identify the modality you're designing for so you can make appropriate design decisions based on the number of sensory inputs students will experience. Here are three examples of evolved unimodal slide design techniques:

slidewire: A short, text-based broadcast that provides an easy, accessible way to push small amounts of information via text-driven layouts

sliderding: An image- and story-driven presentation where some text displayed in the bottom fifth of the slide canvas replaces an audio narration

slidedoc: A term coined by Duarte Design showing how slideware can be used to create a hybrid online viewing experience that lies somewhere between slides as presentation and slides as document

Effective multimodal slides require different design considerations compared to unimodal slides because of modality and context. Most significant, the redundancy effect is irrelevant for unimodal slides because there is no verbal component, so you can add lots more words to the slides than you would for a multimodal context. I mention unimodal slide treatments as a contrast to the focus of this book, though many of the design principles you'll learn will apply in either context.

EXERCISES

1. Critical meditation. Creative work of any kind is an iterative process. The visual process of slide design is unique among instructional materials design because it involves the interplay of your thoughts made visible in interaction with your intended audience, toward goals that you've defined for students.

This lesson challenged a habit that's so widely accepted as to be nearly invisible as a design practice: the idea that you're trying to use one file to do the work of three very different instructional aids: speaker notes, visual aids, and handouts. I suggest taking some time to look back over your years (or perhaps decades) of slide decks and interrogate their efficacy as visual aids, handouts, and speaker notes. Do your designs tend toward one function over the other two? Do they already do a fairly good job as visual aids, or are they serving instead as speaker notes or study guides? Thinking of the things you've learned in this lesson, what old practices are you ready to throw out? Do some of the suggestions still feel impractical? What new practices are you looking forward to adding to your own workflows?

2. Creative uses for slideware. Research the three types of unimodal slide designs mentioned in this lesson: **slidewire** (z.umn.edu/slidewire), **sliderding** (z.umn.edu/sliderding), and **slidedoc** (www.duarte.com/slidedocs). What are the commonalities among these three that you notice? Are some of your slide decks currently serving a role in your courses or course websites that would be more suited to one of these unimodal treatments? Find one of your old decks and convert it to one of the alternative types of learning resources for display on your course website (but don't give a live or recorded lecture from it, which would violate the multimedia principle of redundancy).

Accessible, Functional Slide Decks

This lesson contains almost none of the standard advice about making slides accessible. Typical accessibility advice assumes you're starting with the traditional topic-subtopic slide structure—essentially speaker notes written large on the screen—and that you distribute these slide files directly to students. By contrast, academic slide design suggests preparing a separate, more concise document to distribute to students instead of the slides.   This discussion broadens the idea of accessibility from accommodation to intentionally finding ways to use slides to support attention and to reinforce important concepts. Don't skip this lesson simply because you don't (to your knowledge) have anyone in your class who has a documented need for disability-related accommodation; everyone under the sun has needs that must be supported during teaching and learning.   By the end of this lesson, you'll understand the role of repetition and how it can be useful during a live lecture, and how preview and guidepost slides can help you build this repetition into your slide decks.

You're Already Using Accessible Practices

The good news is that you're likely already employing some accessible best practices in your instructional materials when you practice good written communication:

- Run spell check.

- Spell out acronyms and abbreviations the first time they're used.

- Define technical terms before talking about them in depth.

Some people believe that accessibility means accommodating people with visual and mobility impairments who use adaptive technologies like screen readers to access content. But let's expand that definition to include a host of learning, reading, and attention issues. In this age of information, every one of us has a shortened attention span or problem focusing on one thing or another for a sustained amount of time. Therefore, you're designing for the needs of all your students when you prepare clear, concise, cohesive lectures.

Three Types of Slides: Preview, Guidepost, and Recap

Good lecturers repeat main points often, show where students are in the lecture, and provide many opportunities for interaction with the content. Slides can provide visual reinforcement and cues—all helpful practices during live lectures where students don't have the option to pause and replay, as they would in a recorded talk.

By designing for the functional needs of students during the live lecture event and distilling your messages and designs for clarity, you're improving the learning experience for every single person in your classroom, yourself included. Preview, guidepost, and recap slides all help you remember to reinforce important concepts through repetition.

Preview Slides

Preview slides give a snapshot of the information to come, preparing students for what they're about to learn. Three common applications of preview slides are the graphic organizer, the agenda, and the learning objectives slide.

Graphic Organizer

The graphic organizer illuminates for the novice learner (and perhaps also the instructor) how new information fits within a larger context. Organizing graphics can help make sure that students have a strong foundation on which to build new information. Those who are completely unfamiliar with the topic will use the initial graphic to make sense of subsequent information.

Here is some information from an introductory lecture for the taxonomy unit in a biology course, presented as a list.

Six kingdoms

1. Archaebacteria
2. Eubacteria
3. Protista
4. Plantae
5. Fungi
6. Animalia

The list provides basic information: the six kingdoms and the names of each. Contrast the list presentation with the graphic organizer version in Figure 3.1.

3.1

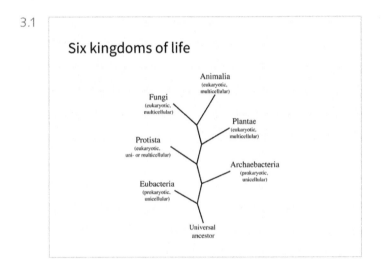

The graphic organizer provides much more information—not only the six kingdoms but also connectors that show that they branch off from a universal ancestor. The spatial arrangement depicts Animalia at the top of the diagram, which signifies a progression from least to most advanced organisms (at least from a cellular point of view). This preview slide provides a more complete overview of the topic, priming students to fill in the details as they listen.

Agenda

A preview slide can be a simple numbered list with an agenda showing the topics or themes that will be covered in the talk. Agenda slides can be made even more effective by incorporating spatial and text-based information about the amount of time that will be devoted to each topic. For example, Figure 3.2 depicts the agenda as a timeline instead of a linear list, with larger and smaller boxes indicating the relative amounts of time that will be dedicated to each part of this talk. It also provides the information in minutes.

The reason this slide works well as a preview slide is twofold. First, it's based on a visual metaphor of a timeline moving left to right. Second, it uses additional visuospatial cues to show the amount of time this lecturer plans to spend on each topic. It can help keep this

3.2

talk on track and can lead to a more organized presentation because you'll have had to make some decisions about the flow of the talk and the length of time spent on each subtopic.

Learning Objectives

Figure 3.3 is a preview slide that graphically depicts a set of learning objectives for an economics lecture on the demise of American whaling.

Showing learning objectives and how they relate to one another within the lecture can help students orient to the main ideas and what they should be listening for, while also helping you check the organization of your presentation. Here the clip art of the sperm whale helps unify the idea that these three reasons all contributed to whaling's demise, while also subtly imparting the idea that sperm whales were the species most hunted during that time.

Guidepost Slides

The slide design equivalent of a text heading in a print-based document, guidepost slides help students know where they are in relation to the larger structure that was promised in the preview. They also visually

3.3

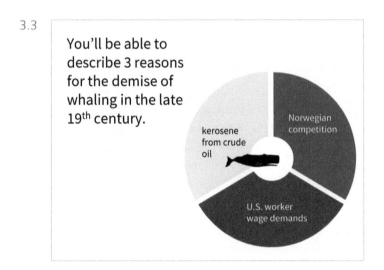

signal that you're moving from one topic to another. Guideposts can be simple text-based slides stating the name of the topic, or they can be a repurposed version of the preview slide. Figure 3.4 shows how four guideposts can be created from the original agenda (Figure 3.2). No additional design work was involved, other than to change the color and text cues to convey "you are here" information for each of the sections. Insert this same slide at the start of each new topic to signal the transition and to remind students of the larger organizational structure.

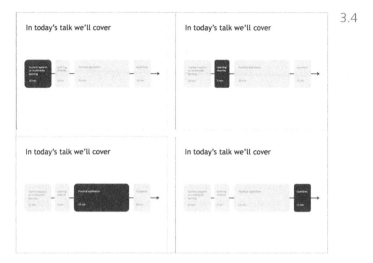

3.4

Guidepost slides support the functional needs of everyone in your audience. They provide mental breaks for students and for you, provide opportunities for questions, and reinforce the main ideas of the lecture through practical repetition. Again, students don't have the benefit of pausing and replaying you during a live lecture, so give them plenty of opportunities to stay "found" through reminders of the organizational structure of your talk.

Recap Slides

Concluding remarks delivered verbally are a helpful end to any lecture. This is the same advice you received when you were learning how to structure other academic writing: tell them what you're about to tell them, tell them, and then tell them what you told them. Consider providing at least one slide that has a visual summary of information you covered, including key ideas and takeaways—a recap slide. A thoughtfully crafted preview slide might even be able to be repurposed here.

Number the Slides

Insert slide numbers for every slide in the deck so students can easily refer to the slide when they have questions. Choose one consistent spot to place this information in an unobtrusive but visible area, perhaps the bottom right corner. (The opposite bottom corner should be reserved for citation information.)

You don't need to enter slide numbers manually. Any robust slideware application should include an automatic slide-numbering feature. Some applications refer to it as page numbering. Aside from saving time, using the slideware to insert the numbers also means the numbering will be updated automatically if you move or delete slides in the deck.

Preparing Slides for Distribution to Students

This section isn't meant to provide step-by-step instructions, but rather to give you an overview of how to prepare a slide file for distribution.

After you start doing academic slide design, you'll likely stop distributing native slide files as often as you once did. For one thing, your slides will no longer simply be a list of bullet points, so they won't be useful as truncated speaker notes. For another, you'll have already created a separate handout that is a concise version of the lecture's main points (see Lesson 4). However, if you do decide to distribute the slide file to students, do these three things to prepare it accessibly:

1. Add unique titles in the title area of each slide, using the predefined layouts. No two slides should have the exact same title (and no slide should include "continued" in the title).

2. Arrange the order of the text boxes so that a screen reader will read them in a logical order. Because you mostly used predefined layouts to add content to the slides (see Lesson 10), the sequencing will only need to be done for objects that were manually added to the slide, such as text boxes and SmartArt. You may need to group some shapes to aid in achieving a logical reading order.

3. Create alternative text for all nontext content. Any text that wasn't entered directly into placeholder fields will need alternative text (including text boxes, interestingly).

Exercises

1. Turn on slide numbering. You don't have to add slide numbers (called "page numbers" in some slideware applications) by hand; figure out how to turn them on and reposition them as necessary in the Slide Master. Remember, it's important to keep the location of slide numbers consistent and visually unobtrusive; this information should be there for the student who is looking for it, but it should be nearly invisible to the student who isn't.

2. Previews and guideposts. Perhaps you already are in the habit of providing agenda slides for your lectures. If not, think about how to add this practice to your slide design workflow. Lesson 16 offers one suggested path. If you already consistently include agenda slides, examine whether the design you usually use for them might also be repurposed as guidepost and recap slides. Insert these wayfinders into one of your decks and try it out on students. What was the effect of a talk where you included wayfinding slides versus one where you didn't? Did you find yourself reorganizing other parts of the lecture based on this activity? Was there any change in the number of questions students asked or how easily they picked up the material? Elicit feedback from students and see whether they believe preview and guidepost slides add value to your lectures.

Accessible,
Functional Handouts

Academic slide design suggests you create a separate, concise document with the discrete purpose of distributing it to students. When you distribute a handout instead of a copy of the slide deck, the standard accessibility advice for slides is replaced with the need to understand how to accessibly format a word processing document.   The purpose of this lesson is to show you how to create an accessible handout, which is arguably much easier than making an accessible slide deck. The practice is more environmental, more portable, and more suited to the task of studying after the lecture is over than the old practice of distributing the whole deck. It also can help you relieve yourself of some of the felt need to create text-heavy slides, because your handout means students will get the main points in a format where being text heavy is okay. But first I need to make the case to you to stop printing handouts directly from the slide application.

Why You Need a Separate Handout

The Print > Handouts feature of your slideware converts your slides into thumbnails that can be printed three-, six-, or even nine-to-a-page (Figure 4.1).

Notice how much wasted space exists in this document and how the content of the slides has been shrunk. When distributed as a print copy, this practice uses a lot of extra paper and suspends the information into image-based text boxes, making it impossible for screen

5/14/16   4.1

Lorem ipsum

- Lorem ipsum dolor sit amet, consectetur adipiscing elit.
- Nam diam mauris, fringilla ut consequat ut, porta nec tortor.
- Maecenas magna risus, consequat sit amet turpis eu, imperdiet cursus neque. Sed finibus, lacus eget bibendum tristique.
- Erat quam ultricies metus, eu malesuada ipsum ipsum ac mauris.

Lorem ipsum

- Lorem ipsum dolor sit amet, consectetur adipiscing elit.
- Nam diam mauris, fringilla ut consequat ut, porta nec tortor.
- Maecenas magna risus, consequat sit amet turpis eu, imperdiet cursus neque. Sed finibus, lacus eget bibendum tristique.
- Erat quam ultricies metus, eu malesuada ipsum ipsum ac mauris.

Lorem ipsum

- Lorem ipsum dolor sit amet, consectetur adipiscing elit.
- Nam diam mauris, fringilla ut consequat ut, porta nec tortor.
- Maecenas magna risus, consequat sit amet turpis eu, imperdiet cursus neque. Sed finibus, lacus eget bibendum tristique.
- Erat quam ultricies metus, eu malesuada ipsum ipsum ac mauris.

1

reader software to access the information. And when distributed electronically as a PDF, it's not suited to modern teaching and learning environments where students might want to type directly on it. But there's an even larger issue here. Thumbnail after thumbnail of shrunk content is all students have to go on when studying alone in their dorm rooms. Taken alone without benefit of instructor voice, the story is lost, the meaning is lost, and the whole lecture is reduced to a series of cryptic clauses missing subject, verb, or other vital sentence parts.

The handout is part of what my colleague, Cris Lopez, terms a "course ecology" of learning aids that also includes lectures, slides, course readings, learning activities, and assessments. Each component has a unique role and purpose in your course. I encourage you to start thinking of the creation of a lecture handout as an activity separate from the creation of script and slides. Although these three products stem from the same planned activity (the live lecture), they're intended for use in separate contexts (the classroom versus students' study spaces). If you really want students to be able to see and study useful information, provide that information in a concise format that they can refer back to at a later date. The purpose of slides is to assist you visually during the lecture. The purpose of a handout is to recap the lecture's main points.

Creating a separate handout aligns with the universal design principle of providing information in multiple formats. For students who have sensory or motor impairments and rely on screen readers or who have other cognitive challenges, such as dyslexia or attention deficit disorders, a carefully prepared handout can provide more efficient access to the main points of your talk than simply providing access to the slides themselves.

You might choose to design the handout either as a worksheet for students to follow along with or as a post-lecture study aid, depending on your instructional goals and the level of your students.

Prepare a Separate Handout That Is Formatted for Accessibility

These are the five core steps required to make word processing documents accessible:

1. Structure the document with section headings and format the headings using paragraph styles.

2. Use the bullet/ordered list tool to format bulleted or numbered lists (rather than manually creating them).

3. Indicate column and row headings in tables.

4. Write descriptive, embedded hyperlinks.

5. Write alternative text for nontext content.

The beautiful thing about these core skills of accessible documents is that they improve the usability of the document for all students, not just those who use adaptive technologies. And they can help you organize your thoughts in a more holistic, structured way. In a word processing document, your thoughts are all in one place, whereas in a slide deck your ideas can get stranded in the Notes area, fractured and distributed across several slides. Structuring a cohesive argument is easier in an application that was meant for composition.

Section Headings

Organize the handout by creating section headings that are easily distinguishable from the rest of the body text using a strong contrast of font size and weight. Style the headings using your word processing program's Paragraph Styles function rather than manually changing the attributes of the text that will serve as headings.

When you use paragraph styles, you make your own life easier: for instance, you can quickly change the appearance of an entire document's worth of headings if you used paragraph styles. You also make the document easier to scan (a desirable quality in information design known as *scannability*) to help students see at a glance how information in the document is organized and help them find what they're looking for. Moreover, paragraph styles make it easier for students who use screen readers; students can use the screen reader software to scan all the headings in a document. By contrast, manually styled section headings are indistinguishable from body text for users of screen readers.

Bulleted and Ordered Lists

Wherever you use a list, use the bullets/ordered lists tool to format it, as opposed to manually creating your own bullets or numbers. This practice also improves scannability. You've likely noticed that the list tool not only inserts the list character (either a bullet or a number) but also formats tabs, spaces, and hanging indents, which creates white space. White space makes it easier for sighted students to scan the information. Using the bullets/ordered lists tool also allows students who use adaptive technologies to scan; screen reader software allows users to isolate and listen separately just to the lists that appear on a page. If you manually format your lists (such as with just a dash and a space), the screen reader won't recognize them as a list.

Tables

Tables should be used to display data rather than as a way to control the layout of your handout. Row and column headers should always be labeled so that the student who can't see the table can tell what information to expect in each cell thereafter. Consult your word processor's table design settings or Help menu to figure out how to specify which row contains the column headings.

Hyperlinks

You can show hyperlinks in two ways: either display the entire text of it (e.g., www.webaim.org) or embed the hyperlink within the words that tell where the link leads (e.g., Migration of Scottish geese lecture notes).

As long as you distribute an electronic version of the handout rather than a physical copy, use the embedded link method, which is more efficient. That way, screen reader users won't have to sit through every character being read aloud in a sometimes-lengthy URL. Embedded links take up less space on a page, making the page less text heavy. However, embedded links will be useless on documents that you distribute as a hard copy, because the link will just look like underlined text.

Properly descriptive, embedded hyperlinks improve both the accessibility and the usability of the link. Aim to create links that tell students exactly what they'll find without having to actually click the link. For example, a descriptive embedded hyperlink named "full reference list" is preferable to "click here for full reference list" where the hyperlink is embedded only in the "click here" portion of the text. Users of screen reader software, which can isolate and read just the hyperlinks that appear on a given page, will be able to tell where the link leads, even out of context of the rest of the sentence. In sum, descriptive, embedded hyperlinks are usually the best solution.

Alternative Text

In order for adaptive technologies like screen readers to be able to read the images in your document, you need to add alternative text, known as *alt text*. You should add alt text to all nontext content, which includes images, graphics, and charts, except decorative elements. It's not necessary to add alt text to decorative elements.

The traditional advice for writing alt text is simply to pretend that you're describing the image for someone who can't see it. But that's not an entirely accurate way to describe this skill. For the alt text, you don't want to simply describe the surface features of the image or graphic (unless this is a photography class and you're discussing technique). Instead, describe the function and content of the graphic. In other words, what is this graphic doing on this page? Why do you want students to look at it? What should they look for? What is the main idea that the graphic is expressing? Write in simple, precise language that doesn't replicate other textual information already in the document. For example, if you have written a caption for the image, you don't also need to add alt text, which would be redundant.

Remember, you'll be doing all this in a word processing application rather than in the slideware and creating rich and efficient learning artifacts in the process.

Exercises

1. Create an outline from an existing deck. It isn't necessary to cut and paste slide by slide into a word processing document in order to get a text-only version of your slides. If your existing slide deck was designed in the traditional topic-subtopic structure, you can easily convert it to an outline that you can then use to create a handout or speaker notes. In PowerPoint, go to File > Save As > .rtf. This process results in a rich text file where the formatting and media have been removed but the text has been preserved in outline form. This handy trick is available in PowerPoint and Google Slides (in Slides: Download as > Plain text file).

2. Create a handout from a text-only outline. This exercise follows on the coattails of the previous .rtf conversion exercise. To make a useful handout, you'll first want to do some rewrites to make sure all the information is in complete sentences and is clear and concise.

Next, add headings (Heading 1, Heading 2, Heading 3, and so on) to structure your document. Use your word processing application's Styles menu rather than manually changing the appearance of the text. As discussed, manually changing the appearance of text isn't helpful for students who use screen readers, because the screen reader won't recognize manually formatted text as a heading.

If your handout includes tables, find where your word processing program lets you indicate row and column headers.

Examine your hyperlinks. Are they embedded in text? Is it possible to tell where the hyperlink goes without having to click on it first? Do the embedded links make sense out of context?

Make sure your bulleted and numbered lists are created using the list tool rather than manually created.

Last, if your handout includes images, add alternative text to those images (you may need to consult the Help menu to figure out how to do this in your particular word processing program).

Fantastic! Now you have an efficient, easily consumable reference and resource to distribute to students.

Unbulleting 1:
Visual Designs
That Aren't Bullets

The use of bullet points (and similarly text-heavy visual treatments) is so common that it's nearly impossible not to think in terms of bullets. Yet bullets-based designs are some of the least effective as a complement to the live lecture. How to think your way toward a new, more effective habit of slide design, when you're surrounded by undeveloped and ineffective examples? The goal of this lesson is to convince you to stop using bullet points or at least to stop using them so often. You'll learn how to start thinking more graphically and less textually. You'll also learn some slide design structures that are naturally less text heavy. Sometimes, though, the best answer is no slide at all.

What's Wrong with Bullet Points?

There's nothing innately wrong with bullet points. In fact, they're the most efficient choice in some contexts (see Lesson 14). However, bullet points are usually a poor choice for a number of reasons. Why?

Bullets Are a Crutch

Bullets encourage you to use the slides as a teleprompter, which can make for a boring lecture. Teleprompter-like slides also may deprive you of the opportunity to be present to the needs of students because you're following the "script" of the projected slides instead.

Bullets Split Attention

As discussed in Lesson 2, it's not possible to read and listen at the same time. When you project bullet points, students are forced to decide whether to read or listen.

Bullets Mimic Organization

Written outlines, of the type we were taught to use in planning a research paper, are great for organizing material for the written page. It's easy to keep track of what level of the hierarchy you're on when you write in a word processing document. However, the strategy of using a hierarchical outline to organize material for a lecture doesn't work. Practically speaking, the outline gets chunked up and segmented, visually separating subordinate topics from the main ideas they support. The resulting design is a twofold problem. First, you get slides that look like Figure 5.1, which would leave students with no visual cues indicating where they are in the hierarchy of steps and numbers. (They'll spend some time wondering, *"Step 4B"? How many steps are there in total? Will all the steps have substeps?*) Second, even if you remove the outline indicators from the slide canvas, it will be harder to keep the information in order if you move the slides around.

Most significantly, lectures aren't like academic papers; they require a different sort of organization, which relies on the cadences of spoken word, repetition of main ideas, and active lecturing techniques in order to be successful. An outline-based presentation created in the same style as a research paper will likely result in a lecture that is more difficult to follow and to remember.

5.1

Step 4B: Analyze sources.

1. Analyze the literature actively
2. Evaluate its relevance to the project: include only selected material directly relevant to the review
3. Create a conceptual framework for the project, including an operational research problem: your research question!
    a. Once you have got a big pile of relevant studies it is difficult not to merely describe one study after another, but this creates an overly descriptive list with few elements of evaluation, critique or narrative structure.

Bullets Are Inadequate to Depict Complex Relationships

Bullet points fail to leverage our natural, nearly instantaneous ability to obtain information from visuospatial arrangement of information, that is, how words and shapes are arranged on a canvas.* See how much more information you're able to obtain—and more quickly—from Maslow's hierarchy depicted visually than from the same information listed as bullet points (Figure 5.2).

* This idea was first articulated by Edward Tufte in his influential and entertaining essay "The Cognitive Style of PowerPoint."

5.2

Maslow's hierarchy of needs

• Physiological needs
• Safety needs
• Love and belonging needs
• Self-esteem
• Self-actualization

Maslow's hierarchy of needs

Self-actualization

Self-esteem

Love and Belonging

Safety

Physiological

Bullets Make It Harder to Show Emphasis

When every piece of information is present on the slide, no one thing is perceived as more or less important than any other thing. Put another way, when you place *all* of your speaking points on the slide, you're unconsciously communicating the message that *everything* is critical.**

** This idea of "powerfully pointing" is from "PowerPoint, Habits of Mind, and Classroom Culture," research on the phenomenological research on the use of PowerPoint in the classroom by Catherine Adams.

Bullets Limit Cognitive Opportunities for Students

When you write out all of the information in the talking points on the slides, you rob students of the ability to engage in the kinesthetic activity of note taking.[*] Why take notes if your instructor is just going to provide a verbatim outline of all the main points later on?

Bullets Are Boring

A wall of text with little visual differentiation is acceptable in a book or journal article—formats that support extended reading—but is difficult to engage with on a screen, especially when that wall of text competes with incoming verbal information.

Worst, bullet points turn the slide into the main event, making you the sidekick.[**] You want to reverse that dynamic. You, the instructor, are the main event, and your slides are your visual assistant. How to get there? Less text-heavy treatments.

The Antidote to Text-Heavy Slides

The antidote to ineffective, text-heavy slides is to train yourself to think more visually and less textually, as my colleague, Alison Link, puts it so concisely. This doesn't mean you need to find a picture of everything you want to depict, which would be impossible to do for many academic subjects and would lead to either decorative or contrived, confusing designs. Instead, start thinking about how you can use the space on the canvas to add meaning, in addition to the words, pictures, charts, graphs and video clips.

You can begin by committing to the idea that each slide should have just one purpose: to communicate just one idea (rather than a text-based list of several ideas). This one purpose could be about content (e.g., the point of this slide is to show students *this*) or function (e.g, the point of this slide is to segue between sections one and two). If you follow this simple advice, you're on your way to thinking and designing more visually and more effectively.

To show you what I mean, first consider the slides in Figure 5.3. The lecturer used the slide canvas to list all the points they wanted to

---

[*]   This idea is borrowed from Catherine Adams's 2008 essay "PowerPoint's Pedagogy." I recommend Adams as foundational reading on the topic of teaching with slides in the classroom.

[**]   A study by Christof Wecker ("Slide Presentations as Speech Suppressors") identified a "speech suppression effect," where students privileged information found on the slides over information delivered orally by the instructor.

5.3

Theme

- The message of the film
- A film means something, whether or not the filmmaker intends it
- Interpretation—supplying meaning—is the job of the audience
- The skeleton, on which action, character and setting, are arranged
- When bare bones are missing; audience knows it

Theme, cont.

- Differ from motif in that themes are ideas conveyed by a film
- Motifs are repeated symbols that represent those ideas
- Leit-motif: reiteration of those themes

Theme, cont.

- Arise from interplay of plot, characters, and the attitude the director takes toward them
- The same story would be given very different themes in the hands of different directors
- Different from director style, which is less visible to amateur viewers

make about film and theme across two slides: a classic example of using slides as a teleprompter. Students will tune out the spoken content while they quickly try to read all of that information before the slide changes. Or they'll spend the time mindlessly copying the bulleted information into their notes so they have it to study from later.

At this point, the design could go in a few different directions, based on the main idea the instructor wants to emphasize.

First, if the essential message of this section is simply to define theme, all that's required is a short descriptive definition. The lecturer can then elaborate.

Another option would be to define the terms through contrast. In this case, the lecturer might contrast "theme" and "motif" on the slide, then elaborate by providing examples of each and explaining their differences (see Figure 5.4).

A third option might be to define theme relationally. Figure 5.5 illustrates a relational definition that is visually communicated through shapes and arrows. The lecturer can then elaborate further.

This skill isn't about dumbing down your slides or your content. What you're trying to do is limit the amount of mental effort students put into learning new information from a text-heavy slide. If they use fewer resources to read a text-heavy slide, they'll have more resources to devote to intrinsically difficult material.

Remember, simple intentionality about what you're communicating visually can breed new insights about what you're communicating verbally and can help ensure that your lectures are focused, on point, and easy to follow. By focusing your own message, you're also helping your students focus.

Slides as Sidekick

Instead of bullet points and other text-heavy designs, effective slides for teaching and learning rely on the interplay between spoken words and graphical representations. Why are slides that contain graphics more effective than text-based slides?

Including simple, graphical visuals can improve your live (and recorded) presentations two ways. From the perspective of planning and delivery, the affordances of graphical visual treatments help you use your slides as sidekick. In all the makeovers in this book, a condition is created that positions the instructor as the main source of information and the slides as the assistant. As you learn these techniques, you'll come to have a different relationship with your slides, and you'll rely on them to illuminate and augment your talk, rather than just read from them.

5.4

Theme is **ideas**

conveyed by the film.

Motif is **repeated symbols**

↓↓↓

that convey the theme.

5.5

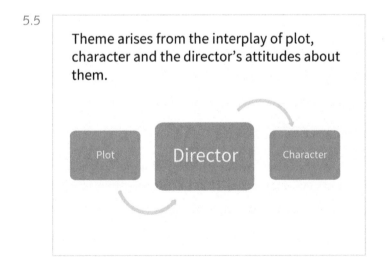

Theme arises from the interplay of plot, character and the director's attitudes about them.

Graphical slides help students apprehend information quickly. You can tell in an instant which one of these bars represents the "most" of something (Figure 5.6). Similarly, you can more quickly ascertain what a velocipede is by looking at a picture of one than by listening to or reading a text-heavy definition. The more quickly students can apprehend the meaning of the slide, the more quickly they can return their attention to you.

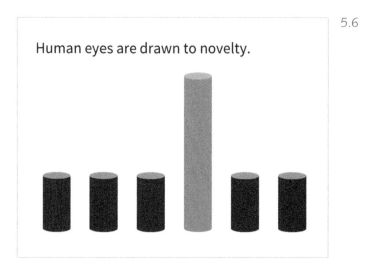

5.6

Human eyes are drawn to novelty.

Some Things You Can Do Instead of Bullet Points

Now to focus on structuring slides that depict relationships rather than list talking points. What might these slides look like? Here are two alternate structures:

- Assertion evidence (see Lesson 7)

- SmartArt treatment (see Lesson 10)

I'll briefly discuss three additional design structures next: text-based treatment, graphics with labels, and full-screen image with title.

Text-Based Treatment

Text-based treatments are just that, slides where the central graphic is comprised of letters. As part of a design repertoire that includes several other design structures, text-based treatments can be an effective means of conveying a main idea. Figure 5.7 is an example.

Graphic with Labels

Sometimes you're lucky enough that the subject matter lends itself to a simple picture of the subject, labeled to show its parts (as in Figure 5.8).

5.7

for **example**

i.e.   ≠   **e.g.**

in other words

5.8

Study these 7 structures that comprise a neural cell.

nucleus

cell body

myelin sheath

dendrite

axon

nodes of Ranvier
(myelin sheath gaps)

axon terminals

Image by NickGorton via Wikimedia Commons

Full-Screen Image with Title

The full-screen image treatment is a useful way to provide some novelty, a visual break, in between slides of complex, heavy content. Figure 5.9 provides an example. (So does Figure 6.4.)

5.9

Some types of information-dense graphics—infographics, concept maps, and mandala-like circular diagrams—may have their uses in slides that are learner controlled, that is, in recorded presentations where students are able to spend as much time as they want on each slide. In fact, any of these designs may be more or less effectively presented, as you'll see in Lesson 13.

In closing, here's a reminder: Lesson 2 introduced the idea that for some subjects and situations, a slide may not be necessary. Now may be a good time to review that lesson if you don't recall the heuristic method for making this determination. Indeed, good designers learn over time what to leave off entirely.

Exercises

1. What's the point? Next time you're sitting in a slide presentation, see if you can remove yourself enough from the content of the talk to analyze the slide designs themselves. Try and articulate the one main point of each of the slides (if it's possible to isolate just one main point per slide). What tensions do you notice when you're doing this exercise? For example, how often are you missing what the speaker is saying? How often are you unable to read the content of the slides as you struggle to listen? Halfway through the talk, switch to focusing just on what the speaker is saying and see if you can imagine what the slide would have to look like if it were to include just one main point per slide. (This exercise is also fun to do with recorded lectures online, perhaps in lieu of a typical evening of pizza and a movie.)

2. Declutter a deck. Dredge up a slide deck from one of your old talks and count the number of slides in the deck. Now perform a high-level pass of the content: go through it, eliminating every slide that is functioning merely as a teleprompter or that tries to accomplish more than one main goal. Preserve and duplicate those slides that could be made more effective by simply dividing the content among several additional slides. Now count the survivors. How many slides do you have left compared to when you started? One of the critiques of a method like this is that you're creating more work for yourself by adding so many more slides to your decks. But in truth what you're likely to find in a decluttering exercise like this is that the ineffective slides you're no longer making balance out with increased effort toward creating better ones.

3. Bulleting backward from a graphic design.
Here's another fun thing you can do on your way to work in the morning. Look around you at whatever graphic designs you see, whether on a billboard or signage posted in your bus or train, and notice the interplay of words and text that forms the designs. Articulate the main message—not the advertiser's call to action ("Buy this lipstick!"), but the message communicated by the design itself ("This new lipstick formula will make you look younger"). Now imagine the design's message as the title of a traditional bullet-pointed slide design. Based on the ad's

visual content—the selected image or images, the typeface, the amount of body copy, what the body copy says, the colors, the tone, the arrangement of all of these things—write five or so bullet points' worth of information supporting the assertion. List them under the title, as you would on a regular one of your slides. Then look back and compare with the original graphic design. Some questions to consider:

- What is the effect of the bullet-pointed version versus the original graphical version?

- What information were you able to obtain from the nontext parts of the ad?

- What information is more efficiently communicated via words versus pictures and vice versa?

The Power
of White Space

Seasoned instructors know that a confident pause judiciously placed in a lecture is the most effective means of getting students to stop what they're doing and look toward the front of the classroom. During a lecture, silence is novel and therefore gets the mind humming with questions, such as, "What will they say next?" or at least, "Why is it so quiet in here all of a sudden?"   White space is the visual analog of silence and is the most effective visual emphasis technique that you have at your disposal. White space clears away all the visual clutter and helps students focus on the one main message of the slide. It differentiates the important from the unimportant (though hopefully you left off the unimportant stuff in the first place). It illuminates rather than occludes, the information you're presenting.   This topic gets its very own lesson because it's that important: I want you to understand the power of white space and to leverage it wherever you can.

White Space as Design Element

How many design elements do you see in Figure 6.1? Some would say one: an orange circle at the bottom right corner of the slide. But I would argue that there are two: the orange circle *and* the gray area that surrounds it.

White space (also referred to as *negative space*) is a term used in art and graphic design to denote areas that contain no other content. White space doesn't need to be white, just blank, but blank doesn't

6.1

mean nothing. Space on a slide isn't an absence. It doesn't need to be filled up. When you start to think about space as one of the design elements on the slide canvas, your designs will drastically improve. Let's apply this space-as-design-element idea to a real life example. Consider the original design in Figure 6.2, meant to accompany a pediatric global health lecture on treating diarrhea in low- and middle-income countries. This slide has a lot of valuable content but hardly any white space, which makes it difficult to focus on any one area.

6.2

● Teach a family member to prepare and give ORS.

● Give to infants and young children using clean spoon or cup. Feeding bottles should not be used.

● Children under 2 year of age should be offered a teaspoonful every 1-2 minutes; older children (and adults) may take sips directly from the cup.

BOX 2: HOW TO PREPARE HOME-MADE ORS SOLUTION

• If ORS sachets are available: dilute one sachet in one litre of safe water

• Otherwise: Add to one litre of safe water:
   — Salt 1/2 small spoon (3.5 grams)
   — Sugar 4 big spoons (40 grams)

And try to compensate for loss of potassium (for example, eat bananas or drink green coconut water)

Salt ? 1/3 small spoon
(new= 75 mEq Na/L vs 90 old)
Sugar ? 2 1/2 big spoons
(new=13.5 g/L vs 20 old))

The makeover (Figure 6.3) is much clearer and more focused because some of the ideas have been reorganized and moved to their own separate slides. It's easier to figure out the main point, and the design feels less overwhelming overall. This is white space at work.

When you start to see white space as part of the design, you'll start to protect it rather than try and plug it up with more information—or worse, decoration.

6.3

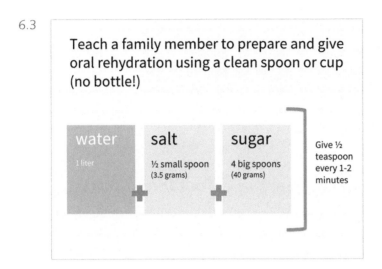

Utilizing Inactive Space

You can also experiment with placing text on top of the inactive space of photographs, as I did with the example in Figure 6.4. The inactive area of photographs is the equivalent of white space: it's the part of the image where the subject is not. Use of the inactive area of an image is one of the visually simplified* methods described by Garr Reynolds in his bestselling book, *Presentation Zen*, which talks at length about how to create this type of slide and shows hundreds of beautiful examples of the technique. Although it may be difficult to utilize this technique over and over for every slide in an academic presentation, the *Zen* method can provide some nice visual variety. When you make this kind of slide, make sure the color and size of text strongly contrast against whatever is going on in the background and that the image complements rather than decorates the text.

---

*   This term is borrowed from Douglas Johnson and Jack Christensen, who did a study comparing student attitudes and outcomes in conditions of either visually simplified and traditional topic-subtopic slide designs ("A Comparison of Simplified–Visually Rich and Traditional Presentation Styles.").

6.4

White Space as a Tool for Emphasis

White space is more effective at calling attention than underlining, bolding, italicizing, coloring, pointing with arrows, or using an effusive number of exclamation marks. Those techniques are visual noise compared to the power of white space. White space naturally forces the eye to move from noncontent toward content. You can't help but be drawn to the novel object on the slide. If you want to bring attention to something, surrounding it with white space is the most effective technique.

Figure 6.5 presents an extended quotation, something often seen on slides. This instructor intends to dissect the quote a little bit, emphasizing each of the ideas it contains. The unintentional effect of all these highlighting techniques is that nothing in particular actually gets visual emphasis; there's too much competition.

To improve this design, you could pick one form of highlighting to help students focus on each part, but the deemphasized elements are still visible and still competing for attention. Look how much more effective this slide becomes when white space is intentionally added to give breathing room around the four edges of the text block (Figure 6.6).

The result is a design that is not only more visually appealing in its simplicity but also more accessible because it helps students focus their attention on the essential. This is key: when you consciously make room for white space, it's much easier to subtract the nonessential; all else becomes extraneous.

6.5

For many students, PowerPoint slide-sets have become an efficient way to prepare for examinations (Frey & Birnbaum, 2002). This presumption is accurate in a very practical sense. **Knowledge that lends itself easily to a PowerPoint slide likely translates well into an examination question.** Whether a teacher is intending it or not, PowerPoint's message of economy to students is: if it does not appear on a slide, it is probably not important because it does not warrant being pointed at powerfully. Here "important" equates with high probability of appearing on a test. The overall effect is the **devaluing of knowledge presented orally** or represented via media other than PowerPoint, for example, on the whiteboard. PowerPoint exercises a powerful presentative sway with students, underlining its authority as the indicative or representational.

-- Catherine Adams

6.6

Whether a teacher is intending it or not,
PowerPoint's message of economy
to students is: if it does not appear on a slide,
it is probably not important because it does not
warrant being pointed at powerfully.

Catherine Adams

Exercise

1. Unclutter a cluttered slide. Visit one of your previously created decks and look at your own use of white space. Take one of your most crowded slides and see what you can do to create more white space while still preserving the intended meaning. Remove decorative elements. Distribute subtopics across several slides. Now reflect on your new, uncluttered design. Would you feel comfortable lecturing with this new slide? How would your presentation style need to change (if at all)? What would your students' reactions be if this were how all the slides in your decks looked?

2. White space expedition. The next time you're at a conference, go on a white-space-finding expedition using your colleagues' slides as your exploration ground. When you spot white space that's being used intentionally for emphasis, take a picture of it, which is your way of commemorating the prize of a successful find. If you think it's an especially inspirational example, file the photo in the visual journal you started back in Lesson 1, and tweet the effective design with hashtag #whitespace, #negativespace, and #hooray.

Unbulleting 2: The Assertion-Evidence Structure

You've never heard of the assertion-evidence (A-E) structure? It's one of the most effective slide designs for teaching and learning. Tell all your friends!   The A-E structure is ideal for the display of data like pies, line graphs, and bar charts. As you'll see in this lesson and in examples throughout the book, it's useful when applied to other kinds of material as well.   The A-E structure has been researched and promoted most extensively by Michael Alley in his book The Craft of Scientific Presentations *and in a number of peer-reviewed journal articles that show its effectiveness at improving recall and retention of information from lectures accompanied by this type of slide. In this lesson you'll learn both how and when to use the A-E structure.*

Assertion-Evidence Structure

Where visuals are used, effective lectures require functional slides that can both handle the complexities of academic subjects and help students remember and retain information. Enter A-E slides, a proven technique that addresses the practical requirements of modern academic lectures.

The A-E structure is pure genius for the fact that it's easy to learn and applicable across subjects, topics, and disciplines. The method is simple. Identify the slide's main idea and write it as a brief sentence at the top of the slide. Then use the remaining space to provide visual evidence that supports the main idea.

The A-E structure not only results in prettier slides but also aligns with research on graphics, memory, and cognition. Slides designed in this way allow students to quickly ascertain what the slide shows, because you're telling them explicitly instead of placing the onus on them to figure out the main point. The best part is that this technique often doesn't even require a complete makeover. Many of your data display slides are likely close to being A-E already; in fact, the A-E structure probably is most impactful when used on slides that display data in graphical forms such as charts and graphs.

This data slide from a marketing lecture (Figure 7.1) is already almost fully conformed to the A-E structure. This slide has one main idea, and clear visual evidence in support of that idea occupies the majority of the slide. To make it into an A-E slide (Figure 7.2), all you

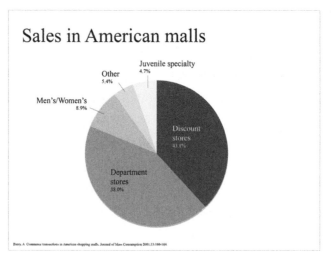

7.1

7.2

need to do is rewrite the phrase heading at the top to explicitly tell students what they're supposed to get from the graphic.

Of course, the conclusions and implications to be drawn from a data display are nuanced and complex. You can talk through those conclusions with the main idea and evidence still displayed behind you for reference, or you can add additional slides with additional assertions, tweaking the display to emphasize different parts of the graphic.

Identify One Main Point Per Slide

As discussed, key to creating successful slides is the ability to identify and articulate the one main point of the slide. Most text-heavy, bulleted slide designs contain lots of points—sometimes in support of the same main idea, sometimes not, often because the instructor was writing the lecture in the presentation software, rather than in a word processing document (see Lesson 16 for a number of good reasons not to plan lectures that way). Writing is thinking, and we all need to do a lot of writing (thinking) in order to uncover our main points.

Take a look at Figure 7.3. The history of early Christianity is a huge topic, and this designer tried to fit a lot of it into a 10 x 7.5-inch space. On closer examination, this slide isn't about the early Christian church after all, but actually about the work of the apostle Paul. Take a look at the last bullet in the first section: "If not for Paul, Christianity may have remained a branch of Judaism." That statement appears to be the culmination of

7.3

Early Christian Church

ᘓ

Saul of Tarsus
- ᘓ Became Paul the Apostle
- ᘓ Missions throughout Asia Minor
- ᘓ Previously opposed idea of Jesus as Messiah
- ᘓ Saw Jesus on way to Damascus, became Christian (Conversion)
- ᘓ Epistles (letters) became part of the new testament
- ᘓ Established Christian churches throughout Mediterranean
- ᘓ Taught mostly in Jewish communities
- ᘓ If not for Paul, Christianity may have remained a branch of Judaism

Roman religious persecution
- ᘓ Rulers began to see Christianity as a threat
- ᘓ by AD 300, about 10 percent of Romans were Christian

the thinking behind the other bullets, and it's certainly the most pro-vocative. What would this slide look like if that assertion were moved to the top of the slide and built out with visual evidence?

Spare students the lead-up to the main points. Instead, identify one main point per slide, which will be easier to illuminate, easier to organize, and easier to remember. After you do that, you're free to continue to talk from that main idea while verbally providing supporting arguments.

Nondata Examples of the A-E Structure

Think of A-E as one among many in your bag of design tools and a go-to strategy when you find yourself leaning toward writing up a list of bullet points to place on a slide. What about topics that aren't data driven?

Example 1: Effective Comparison

The slide in Figure 7.4 displays a lot of text that the instructor wants to remember to mention. The image in the corner doesn't help students learn about characteristics of the moon; currently it functions as decoration and space filler.

To apply the A-E structure, first identify the real point of this slide, which is that the near side of the moon is characterized by the lunar maria. This point is stated in the title section of the slide. The rest of the body text is elaborative and can be moved to the speaker notes area of the slide (not shown). The image is then promoted to the center of the slide (Figure 7.5) and by its central position makes it clear to students that the image is significant.

For students who don't know what lunar maria are, it will be easier to distinguish what they are from what they are not. For this reason, a second image is added for comparison. This step juxtaposes a new image of the far side of the moon with the original near side image. Add arrows to highlight the lunar maria, and the result is a slide that creates meaning through a combination of supportive images that interact with the text. Figure 7.6 shows the completed makeover.

The A-E structure can improve the quality of your lectures by forcing you to identify main points and to introduce them to students in an active way.[*]

---

[*]   The articulation of the main point in an active way is terminology borrowed from Michael Alley et al., "How the Design of Headlines in Presentation Slides Affects Audience Retention."

7.4

Near side of moon

- Moon hemisphere always seen from earth
- Sometimes illuminated by earthshine
- Dark spots are high in iron
- First mapped early 17th cent., early astronomers thought they were bodies of water
- Lunar maria (Latin for "sea")

7.5

The near side of the moon is characterized by lunar maria, low-lying areas high in iron.

7.6

The near side of the moon is characterized by lunar maria, low-lying areas high in iron.

Near side   Far side

Assertion-Evidence Misinterpreted

The assertion-evidence structure can be misinterpreted, that is, not used to best effect. The A-E slide in Figure 7.7 about the 1883 Krakatoa eruption shows an ineffective assertion (multiple massive effects are alluded to, which would require multiple pieces of visual evidence in order to prove) and poorly selected evidence. In fact, the picture of the islands seems to prove some different assertion alltogether, perhaps something about the size of the islands following the eruptions. A-E slides are most effective when the chosen evidence illuminates the main point, which is discussed at length in upcoming lessons.

7.7

Example 2: Evocative Image

The slide shown in Figure 7.8 uses the traditional topic-subtopic slide structure. Although the slide lists characteristics of a peat bog and the text explains how those characteristics contribute to the formation of bog bodies, students might have trouble identifying the main idea and might focus on reading the text rather than listening.

An A-E makeover first articulates the main idea: that microbial activity is inhibited in peat bogs, resulting in preservation of organic material. Place that main idea in the title area at the top of the slide and pair it with an image that illustrates the concept (as in Figure 7.9).

Rewritten as an assertion, the main idea isn't just another fact; it's a statement that describes cause and effect. The photograph of the

7.8

Bog bodies

- Peat bogs are made of *Sphagnum* moss
- Anaerobic environment and tannic acids
- Inhibits growth of microbes
- Can result in preservation of organic material
- Tollund man

7.9

Anaerobic environment and tannic acids in peat bogs inhibit microbial growth, preserving organic material.

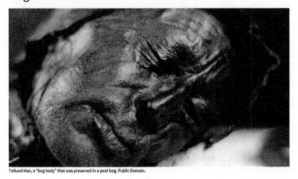

Tollund Man, a "bog body" that was preserved in a peat bog. Public Domain.

Tollund Man answers students' natural question: "What does a bog body look like?" The evocative image also communicates better than words that bog bodies can be uncannily well preserved. Look at those amazing wrinkles!

The success of an A-E slide rests partially on successful selection of strong visual evidence to support the main point. This selection is dependent on your instructional goals and on the level of the students. For example, more advanced students who already know what a bog body looks like might benefit instead from a different graphic, perhaps one that shows the anaerobic action at work in the preservation of bog bodies.

Label Graphics and Their Composite Parts

Complex visual evidence may require additional supports, such as labels, to aid interpretation. For guidance on this issue, we turn to multimedia learning theory and, specifically, the spatial contiguity principle, which suggests that the best way to provide additional interpretative information within a graphical display is to place labels on or as close to the graphic as possible.* Instead of providing a key or legend (as in the top of Figure 7.10), label the parts of the graphic directly (as in the bottom of Figure 7.10). Asking students to hold information from a key or legend in working memory while matching it up with information in the graphic taxes mental resources.

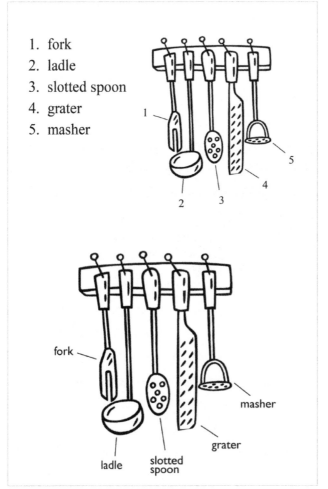

7.10

1. fork
2. ladle
3. slotted spoon
4. grater
5. masher

---

* In a presentation for the Harvard Initiative for Teaching and Learning ("Research-Based Principles for Multimedia Learning"), Richard Mayer lists twenty-two studies that show strong evidence for the spatial contiguity principle.

Exercises

1. Point and purpose. As we've been discussing, each slide should have either a functional (preview, guidepost, recap) or content-related reason for being a part of your deck. Open three or four of your older slide decks and find the slides that contain the most text. Examine the text closely. Identify the reason you made each slide, keeping a tally. Some of these likely were purely administrative (such as, "Students: prepare for Tuesday's quiz!"), but the rest should have either a functional or content purpose. Of the slides in your typical deck, how many are functional? How many are content? Healthy slide decks should have some of both, and you should be able to articulate the purpose of each.

2. Slide makeover. Although it extends well to other situations, the A-E structure is optimal for explaining slides that have a data display. Look back through your existing slide decks and identify at least one slide that displays some data in a chart, graph, or table, and at least one slide that contains a graphic. Examine the heading (title) you originally wrote. Chances are it was written as a vague phrase that required viewers to come up with their own ideas about what the graphic showed. Rewrite this vague title in a more descriptive way. Forget the arbitrary guidelines you've heard governing number and placement of words on slides (e.g., "No more than eight words per line and four lines per slide"). Break from the pattern of a phrase-based heading and actually write a full (but concise) sentence up top. This exercise helps you develop a habit of writing assertions that focus the main point of each slide while also displaying the most important ideas that you want your students to remember from those slides.

Selecting
Illuminative Visuals

Have you ever been tempted to add decorative elements to your slides because you were afraid that otherwise they would look boring? Don't do it. Although it may be tempting to think that adding decorative elements will help gain students' attention, decorations have the opposite effect. As discussed in previous lessons, your slides are meant to function as visual aids in support of your presentation. When you add decorative elements, you're actually distracting students from the important information on the slide, and worse, from your presentation. The choice of visuals and media is, therefore, a crucial visual literacy skill. In this lesson, we'll talk about how to identify and eliminate decoration, and how to choose graphics that illuminate the important points you make in your lectures. By the end of the lesson, you'll have a deeper understanding of the interplay of visual and verbal information and be able to create presentation slides where visual and verbal inform each other. And I hope you'll have increased confidence that your slide content can stand alone without decoration.

Illuminative, Not Decorative
Visual Treatments

Much research demonstrates that decorative graphics interfere with learning. The literature on the coherence principle of multimedia learning theory describes this phenomenon.* When decoration is present, students attend to the decoration in addition to the content, trying to figure out where the critical information is located. That seemingly innocuous clip art you include on text-heavy slides to jazz things up actually fragments students' attention. Additionally, decoration is difficult to do well and can make your slides look unintentionally amateurish.

A frequent offender in this category is the slick, corporate-looking pabulum that's offered on stock photo websites—stuffy pictures of people in suits sitting in boardrooms looking excited about fake charts. Those types of pictures are visual junk and have no place on instructional slides, even if you teach in a business school.

An equally bad idea is to add graphics simply because you think the space looks empty. Remember that white space is your secret weapon for good design.

What actually holds students' attention is genuine interest in the content—caused by listening to you, the expert. When you're passionate about your subject matter, when you're willing to share with students the reasons you find the subject so interesting, when you present the material in an organized way at an appropriate pace with plenty of interactive opportunities, your students will pay attention.

How to Detect Decoration

Here's a simple test to determine whether text, images, lines, and shapes are acting as decoration: articulate the meta-purpose of the graphic. For example, "This diagram supports the main assertion of this slide, which is to show the primary classifications of traditional Maori instruments." Or, "This arrow calls attention to the V4 area of the visual cortex in the human brain, which perceives color and form."

If you aren't able to articulate a clear purpose that serves teaching and learning, that element is probably serving a decorative function and should be removed.

*   See the *Cambridge Handbook of Multimedia Learning*—specifically, chapter 12, "Principles for Reducing Extraneous Processing in Multimedia Learning: Coherence, Signaling, Redundancy, Spatial Contiguity and Temporal Contiguity"—for a summary of several decades of research on the effect of seductive details in multimedia learning.

Institutional Logos

Your institutional marketing department may have furnished you with a slide template where the logo appears on the bottom of every slide. But if you think about it, institutional logos are another form of decoration.

I encourage you to exercise your academic freedom and use your own blank template, one that displays your institutional logo only on the first and last slides in the deck. Your students don't need to be reminded what school they go to. Even when you're speaking at a conference, including the logo on the first and last slides should be sufficient for the audience to remember where you're from (though see the sidebar "Conference Hack: They're Tweeting My Slides!" in Lesson 15). Decoration, whether branding or clip art, detracts from students' limited supply of attentional resources and takes up valuable screen real estate.

Start with a Blank Canvas:
Strip the Theme

Prebuilt themes are a feature of presentation software that applies a particular styling (color, font, layout, and decoration) to all the slides in your deck. I suggest you not use them.

Themes unintentionally communicate a tone that rarely matches the content of serious academic presentations. Each of the themes shown in the themes montage in Figure 8.1 has its own emotional vibe

8.1

that would only be appropriate in a narrow set of circumstances. Emotional tone is difficult to do well, and it can hamper your ability to create effective arrangements because you have to add your content in around the fluff and decoration.

With hard-to-read text styling, such as reflections, drop shadows, or all caps case, themes often create accessibility problems as well.

Strip your decks entirely of theme and start from a blank canvas. Either the light (white) or the dark (black) version of the plain theme can be equally effective, though it may be easier for students to view contrasts between text and background if you choose the dark background anytime you know you'll be speaking in a low-lit or large room like a conference ballroom. The important thing is that you control the look and feel of the deck. Let your own creativity thrive and your content be the main event.

Make It Meaningful

Seeing what you're saying and hearing what you're saying helps students encode information two ways. Visuals should function as proof of what you're saying. In other words, the visuals should augment, not simply replicate or illustrate, your verbally delivered material.

You're striving for a condition of illumination here—a synergy between the visual and the aural that creates an aha! moment of understanding.

Selecting visual evidence is the easiest place to misstep. Why? Because we're so used to seeing examples of poorly selected visuals and because the current culture of teaching and learning expects that decks include a slide for every point the presenter will make. But a lot is at stake: poor visual choices can result in ineffective slides that do nothing to help students understand, integrate, and remember information. Worse, poorly selected visuals may distract the learner completely from what you're trying to say. Let's take a look at some graphical choices done wrong and then done right.

The slide in Figure 8.2 defines serial recall position, a concept from cognitive psychology, which explains how people tend to remember the first and last items in a list more readily than items mentioned in the middle. A typical slide design for depicting this concept might include bullet points and an accompanying graphic.

Let's focus on the image that was selected for this slide. Elephants are said to have remarkable long-term memory, and memory is kind of what's being talked about here, but the picture is an ineffective

8.2

Serial position in memory recall

- Primacy and recency effects
- Number of items on the list matters
- First described by Hermann Ebbinghaus in 1885

Godot13 via Wikimedia Commons

choice. The student needs to know that bit of folklore in order to understand why the instructor placed this image on the slide. The elephant image functions as decoration and doesn't make a meaningful contribution to students' understanding of the concept.

Figure 8.3 shows another attempt. The text is the same, but the image has changed. This image is even less useful, because it depicts computer rather than human memory. This image also is purely decorative and doesn't contribute toward meaning. Students will need to spend some time making sense of the relationship between the image and the slide rather than focusing on the main point.

8.3

Serial position in memory recall

- Primacy and recency effects
- Number of items on the list matters
- First described by Hermann Ebbinghaus in 1885

Public Domain

Figure 8.4 uses a stock photo image typical of the results of an internet image search for "memory," depicting a person who has trouble remembering. Again, this image doesn't reinforce the idea of serial positioning.

8.4

Serial position in memory recall

- Primacy and recency effects
- Number of items on the list matters
- First described by Hermann Ebbinghaus in 1885

What else can we try? Figure 8.5 uses clip art that relies on a cultural understanding of the concept of tying a string around one's finger to help them remember to do something. Even for students who possess this cultural understanding, the graphic evokes the general concept of "memory" in general and not the concept of serial position.

8.5

Serial position in memory recall

- Primacy and recency effects
- Number of items on the list matters
- First described by Hermann Ebbinghaus in 1885

Here's one more undeveloped example. Figure 8.6 presents a scientific-looking illustration of the brain; this slide is talking about human memory, after all. The problem with this graphic is that it depicts the *parts* of the brain rather than serial positioning, which is a *phenomenon* of the brain. Although it looks science-like, this graphic is just functioning as decoration.

8.6

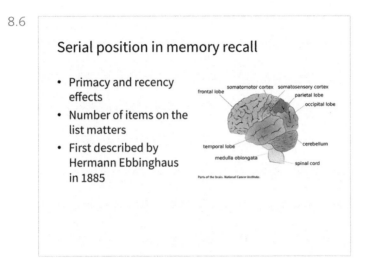

Let's make this slide over using an illuminative graphic.

Figure 8.7 not only depicts the idea of serial position but also illustrates three phases of the concept. This well-chosen graphic gives students a mental construct to understand both what serial position

8.7

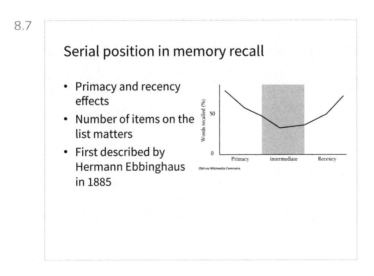

is *and* how it operates. Because this graphic is directly connected to the concept, students now have a better chance at apprehending and remembering. The serial position image is now appropriately illuminative.

However, this slide still includes the type of bullet points that we're trying to avoid—imprecise phrases that serve as talking points for the instructor. This slide can be further improved by applying the A-E technique.

In the makeover (Figure 8.8), the carefully chosen evidence is enlarged and is accompanied by a definitional assertion. Students will have an even easier time apprehending the message of this slide and carrying the information forward. The bullets have been moved to the speaker notes for the instructor to talk through verbally.

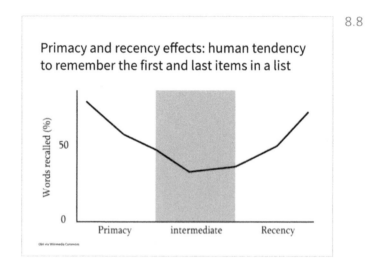

8.8

Did this section feel a little tedious? It was so on purpose; people make these kinds of mistakes all the time, and I wanted to show you one by one the most common places people tend to misstep when choosing visuals. But now you know to be intentional about selecting graphics and video clips so that they're interdependent with your message, not decorative or redundant to it.

An Illuminative Makeover

The challenge to achieving illuminative graphics can sometimes be that the subject matter doesn't seem to lend itself well to graphical treatments. Representing theories through slides can be especially challenging. What can we do?

Take a look at the slide in Figure 8.9, taken from a lecture on animal behavior. The slide designer has introduced the concept of filial imprinting along with a picture of the scientist, Konrad Lorenz, who described it.

The selection of a photo of the scientist as a visual for the slide is somewhat understandable. Using a picture of a person is easier than figuring out the best way to visually depict an aspect of a theory. However, the main point of this slide is the theory, not the theorist, and looking at a picture of him doesn't reinforce the concept of filial imprinting. This image currently functions as decoration.

8.9

Let's take a look at the makeover in Figure 8.10.

8.10

This photo illustrates filial imprinting in action with the ducks following closely behind the scientist who they believe to be their mother (and also happens to feature Dr. Lorenz himself). The image illuminates the concept of filial imprinting. Students will remember the concept more easily.

Be your own editor and resist the temptation to fill white space on your slides by adding unrelated or tangentially related graphics. Your slides should include only the essentials, so that every visible element either carries information or helps your students organize incoming information.

Exercises

1. Decoration or not? Here's another chance to walk around in your daily life looking at graphic designs. I challenge you to find anything in a professionally designed piece, be it a brochure, billboard, or business card that serves as mere decoration. If you do spot something that looks entirely decorative in an advertisement or other visual display, look closer. Can you find another reason that element was included? Chances are that even something that looks decorative initially is there for a reason, perhaps to guide your eye to the most important parts of the design. In short, designers don't decorate.

2. Lessons from documentary programming. Watch a few episodes of an instructional or documentary television program such as the *Mayday: Airplane Crash Investigation* series by Cineflix Productions. You can find full episodes on YouTube. Pay attention to the ways in which instructional graphics and animations are used in combination with the narrator's voice and the way footage of survivor interviews, computer-generated reenactments, and other video is intermixed to create a compelling narrative. Consider these questions as you watch.

- What types of information are instructional graphics and animations used to communicate?

- Do the instructional graphics and animations help the viewer understand the voiceover narration or are they merely decorative?

- What lessons might you take from studying how these instructional graphics are used in relation to your own selections of appropriate visual images?

In addition to helping you come to terms with your mortality, this exercise can help you build an awareness of the ways in which multimedia—properly applied—can enhance the learning experience.

3. Textbook illustrations. Grab your favorite textbook (I know you have one) and select a couple of pages to review that include graphics such as images, diagrams, graphs, and charts. Consider these questions.

- When are diagrams used to reinforce ideas expressed through text? How do diagrams make the meaning of text clearer and easier to understand?

- When are images used, versus line drawings? How do they reinforce or augment the text? Do all images or drawings contribute meaning, or can you find some that are purely decorative?

- When there is only text and no graphics, is the meaning of the text clear enough? What graphics might be used to make the meaning even clearer?

Unbulleting 3: Communicating Meaning through Spatial Positioning

You don't need to be an artist or even a particularly creative person in order to communicate visually via slides. You only need to have spent some time developing your visuospatial muscles. You can communicate so much through the shapes and lines you display on your slides and also through how you arrange them in relation to one another. The goal of this last lesson in the "unbulleting" series is to help you discover how much you already know about visuospatial communication and to give you some inspiration to leverage those tools in your own designs. In this lesson, you'll learn some techniques for how to arrange objects and how to use lines and shapes to communicate ideas, which can further empower you to move away from bullet points.

Arranging Objects and Shapes to Communicate Meaning

Thanks to the affordances of human visual perception and our evolutionary history as symbolic thinkers and meaning makers, it's possible to communicate thousands of concepts and ideas through the arrangement of simple shapes and lines on a slide. Here are some things that the arrangement of graphics on a slide can communicate.

- **Hierarchy:** What is most important? Least important?

- **Relationship:** What belongs to what? What's included? What's excluded?

- **Process or sequence:** What came first? What are the steps?

- **Anomalies:** What is the typical scenario or state? What might look different or go awry?

Students will impose their own pattern-finding and meaning-making processes on incoming information. The meaning they draw from the visuals you design will also be influenced by their prior knowledge of the topic, their level of visual literacy, the cultural context, and even their mood on the day of the lecture. Your job as an expert is to find the best design that helps them select, organize, and integrate new information—the three key encoding processes in multimedia learning (see Lesson 2).

Let's take a look at some techniques you can use to communicate meaning through positioning. You'll likely discover you already know and understand most of them intuitively.

Designing with SmartArt

Some concepts and relationships may seem too abstract to be able to present visually, but PowerPoint's SmartArt tool can give you inspiration and help you build these kinds of graphics that use spatial positioning to communicate. (As of this writing, no equivalent to this powerful tool exists in Keynote, LibreOffice Impress, or Google Slides, though third-party tools exist that can accomplish similar effects.) SmartArt also provides screen tips to help you choose the type of graphic that's most appropriate for your content, and all you have to do is enter your own text and images. When you're done using the SmartArt builder wizard, you can convert the graphic to shapes and make additional stylistic customizations.

Figure 9.1 depicts just a few of the types of relationships that SmartArt can help you show: divergent concepts, cycles, hierarchies, and inputs with results. Note how the positioning of simple shapes in each of these arrangements works to communicate broader concepts. Getting adept at SmartArt may take a bit of experimentation, but it will open new possibilities for expressing and communicating your ideas.

9.1

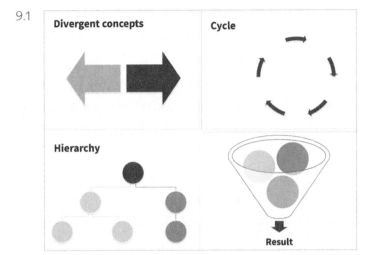

Consistent Style

Your slides will look more cohesive (and hence, more professional) when you decide on one consistent style for the graphics in your decks. In this context, style refers to the surface features that comprise the appearance of the shapes. Let's look at some examples. Consider the difference between the graphics depicted on the left and right of Figure 9.2. Both graphics are comprised of the same shapes and spatial arrangement. However, the one on the left has a flat style; it looks like ink on a page. By contrast, the one on the right has a raised-edge, glossy effect that gives it a 3-D appearance, like glue

9.2

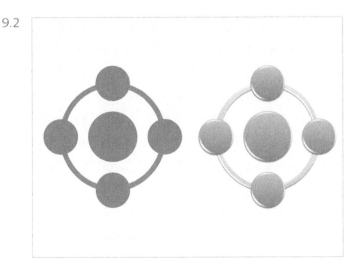

poured on a nonporous surface. Notice how the different surface features create distinct visual effects. Comparing just two graphics, this difference can feel inconsequential, but over the course of an entire slide deck, the use of multiple styles can make the whole thing look like a hodgepodge.

A second example uses more iconic (picturelike) graphics. The top row of pictures in Figure 9.3 shows four different methods for representing a heart, while the bottom row shows glasses of red wine in varying styles.

9.3

How would you go about matching each wine with each heart, just based on graphic style? Completing this exercise requires that you look beyond the shape and meaning of the object and focus on surface features—the thickness of lines, the evenness or unevenness of shapes, the shadows, and the 3D effects.

Becoming more aware of surface features will help you choose consistent graphics, which can lead to a more cohesive slide deck. Taking the time to articulate a graphic style also can save you time; you'll have narrowed your decisions in a field of infinite choice.

Lines

The line is thin but powerful. Eyes follow lines. A sure way to ensure students' eyes follow a specific path is to draw a line, as we can't help but want to see where it leads. Our eyes also attempt to make meaning from lines. Be careful about using lines in your slides, because they may unintentionally disrupt the flow of a design or communicate a false separation between items. For example, a line drawn between shapes separates them into groups. That's why lines that divide the slide title from the rest of the content are a bad idea (as in Figure 9.4).

Use lines to show connections or to communicate something about the quality of the connection. For example, a solid line can suggest a strong link between two shapes, where a dotted line might suggest a weaker, or perhaps temporary, connection (Figure 9.5). A jagged line may suggest a tense or brittle relationship between items.

9.4

Insecticide-treated bednets also work in

1. Leishmaniasis
2. Japanese encephalitis
3. Lymphatic filariasis
4. Chagas disease
5. Head lice & bed bugs
6. All of the above
7. None of the above

9.5

Project management is part of an ecosystem of roles.

Marketing and promotions

External stakeholders

Business owner

User interface specialist

Project manager

Content lead

Technical lead

— Primary
.... Secondary

Lines also can communicate a story, progression, or path. Figure 9.6 shows how a line can lead the eye through a process.

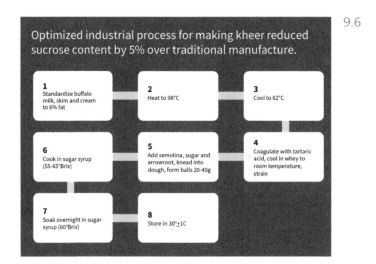

Forms that appear on a horizontal line indicate a continuum of states (Figure 9.7), a timeline (see Figure 10.12), or a scale (Figure 9.8). Flat lines create a feeling of stability, whereas lines that go up or down suggest an increase, decrease, or other unstable condition.

Lines also have discipline-specific meanings. A line used in a diagram in an electrical engineering context may have a different

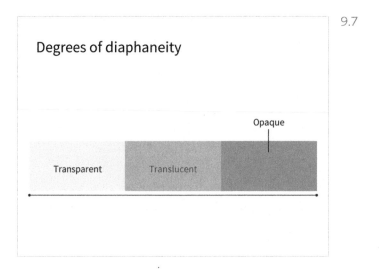

meaning than the ones discussed here. How are lines used in your discipline? How might you use them to communicate complex ideas in your subject matter?

9.8

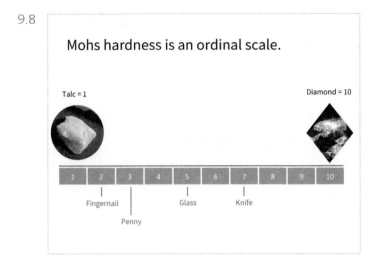

Shapes

We perceive closed or nearly closed lines as shapes. Shapes are useful in visual communication not only for what they include or enclose but also for what they exclude (Figure 9.9).

9.9

Shapes, such as thought bubbles, arrows, and hearts, have symbolic meaning that is culturally or contextually imposed (Figure 9.10). Be prepared that not all students may have the visual literacy to understand the significance of any of these shapes in the context of a particular message. For reasons of both accessibility and usability, you should be able to talk through your designs during your lecture to explain their arrangement and meaning.

9.10

Shape and Emotion

You can use shapes in an intentional way to convey emotion or quality, either positive or negative, depending on context. Figure 9.11 shows the same schematic drawing represented two ways.

Consider the subtle yet distinct effects in visual tone. Even the simple decision to use all rounded shapes or all angular shapes can have an impact on the overall experience of your slide designs.

Use Strong Shape Contrasts

A contrast of size between shapes can be useful in showing what is more dominant, more important, or more influential, or what represents a larger quantity as part of a comparison. If you need students to be able to discern the difference between two areas, make sure the characteristics of the shapes are adequately different. Make one very big

9.11

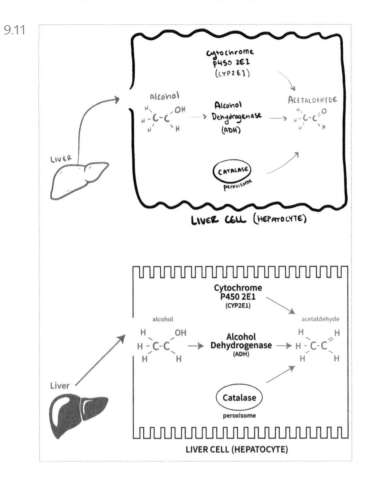

and the other much smaller. In cases where manipulating size isn't possible, add a distinct texture or pattern to help differentiate. Make it as easy as possible to distinguish differences.

Gestalt Principles

Gestalt theory was first described by Austrian and German psychologists in the late 1800s to show how we make sense of visual information. In the modern era these phenomena have been corroborated in the field of neuroscience. The Gestalt principles show how meaning is created by the placement of objects near or far apart from each other. Although there are eight, ten, or twelve principles (and counting), two that are particularly useful for everyday visual communication tasks are proximity and similarity.

Proximity

Objects placed close to one another indicate that they belong to the same category or set. By the same token, objects placed apart from the group are perceived as different. Even though each type of feminism is depicted by a different color in Figure 9.12, we naturally perceive that difference, Marxist and liberal feminisms have something in common with each other and therefore belong together when viewed through the lens of theoretical divide.

In Figure 9.13, text and images that represent types of biomes are placed proximally to their typical geographic locations across the globe.

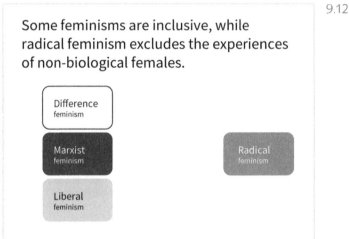

9.12

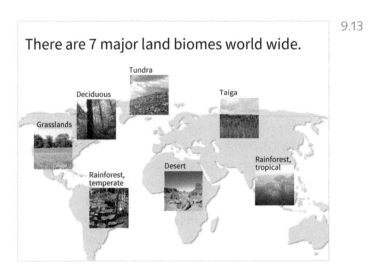

9.13

For example, students will instantly perceive from looking at this slide that the taiga biome is generally located across the northern part of the European continent. Proximity is such an integral part of the human perceptual experience that you probably use it all the time. Now that you know the concept, you can use it strategically.

Similarity

Items that appear to share surface features in common, such as the same size, shape, or color, are likely to be perceived as related to each other. This is the Gestalt principle of similarity. By the same token, dissimilar items will most likely be perceived as not being related. In Figure 9.14, which presents an alphabetical list of variants of feminisms, those variants categorized as difference feminisms are presented with a color block. Students will perceive that the difference feminisms are part of the same group, even though the members of the group aren't located near each other.

9.14

Variants of difference feminism versus other feminisms	Amazon	Indigenous	Postmodern
	Analytical	Individualist	Radical
	Anarchist	Labor	Religious
	Anti-pornography	Liberal	Separatist
	Atheist	Lipstick	Sex-positive
	Black	Marxist	Social
	Chicana	Material	Socialist
	Cultural	Maternal	Standpoint
Difference	Cyber	Native American	Transfeminist
Other	Difference	Neo	Transnational
	Equality	New	Vegetarian Eco
	Fat	Post-structuralist	Womanism
	Global	Postcolonial	
	Hip hop	Postfeminist	

When relying on the principle of similarity to communicate relatedness or unrelatedness, make sure the contrast between the two groups is strong so that students can perceive the differences as effortlessly as possible.

Exercises

1. Gestalt image hunt. The point of this lesson really was to show you some visual understandings that you already possess and to provide some inspiration for other things you could do on your slides instead of bullet points. But the body of work on the topic of Gestalt makes an interesting visual study and can help raise your awareness of the thousand ingenious designs you pass by every day. Take a few minutes to search the internet for the Gestalt principles; as discussed, there are more than just the ones discussed here. You'll start to see the Gestalt principles at work in a variety of graphic designs. As you begin to notice more and more of them, quiz yourself and see if you can name the principle at work. Place a few of your favorites in your visual journal, if the mood strikes you.

2. Get the squint test. Andrew Abela, PhD, who wrote *Advanced Presentations by Design*, offers free for download a useful set of thirty-six slide layouts that pass what he calls the "squint test." As of this writing, the layouts are available at www.powerframeworks.com/squint-test. The idea is the same as what we've been talking about: students ought to be able to figure out the message of the slide before they even read the words; they should get clues to the concepts and relationships simply by the positioning of elements on the slide. Go take a look at the squint test designs. What inspiration can you draw from this collection? Which ones might be useful for concepts you teach?

Layout and Composition

In Lesson 9 we examined the ways you can select and arrange simple shapes
and lines to communicate complex ideas. This lesson broadens the conversation,
delving more deeply into layout and composition and the additional meaning-
making opportunities you have when you consider not just the relationships between
individual elements on a slide, but also the slide canvas as a whole.   Although
layout and composition are sometimes used interchangeably, there's a practical
reason to explicitly define these terms in the context of this discussion. Layout
here is a functional term, referring to the way presentation software works.
Composition, on the other hand, is a sophisticated concept in art and design having
to do with how you position elements on the canvas. Composition has implications
for both the viewer's perceptual experience and understanding of a design.
This lesson brings together concepts from both those conversations in order to
provide practical guidance in answer to the question: How do you arrange graphics,
shapes, and text?   By the end of this lesson, you'll be able to make more reasoned,
less arbitrary decisions about where to put things on the slide canvas.

Three Ways Layout and Composition Influence Meaning

The terms *layout* and *composition* aren't interchangeable in this lesson.
Most robust presentation softwares include predefined layouts to help

you place content on slides, and you should use those layouts wherever possible, instead of adding content with text boxes.

One of the ways layouts influence meaning is by controlling the position and visual appearance of content, helping you create consistency and cohesion. As discussed, consistency and cohesion support students' ability to learn from your slides because they come to predict how information will be displayed.

A second way layout and composition influences meaning is through hierarchy. Hierarchy of elements in the composition influences which part of the design vies for the viewer's attention. You can control the way your students perceive your designs two ways: by attending to the qualities of the objects and by where you place them on the slide. By qualities I'm talking about how big, small, bold, or bright they are. Graphic designers call this combination of phenomena visual hierarchy.

Finally, the placement of elements on the slide canvas influences the meaning that viewers take from the composition. What does it mean to place an object on the left versus the right side of the canvas, top or bottom, center or margin? Certain culturally defined understandings underlie compositional decisions. Even if students aren't totally conscious of these understandings, you increase the sophistication and effectiveness of your designs when you have some awareness of these meanings.*

Let's discuss each of these influences in more detail.

Common Composition Issues

The next slides show several common composition issues.

- Figure 10.1 indicates no point of entry for the eye.

- Figure 10.2 has no focal point. In fact it has several elements competing for that status.

- Figure 10.3 presents information in a way that conflicts with understood norms (backward motion, not forward).

---

* The framing of this lesson, particularly the discussion of information value related to object placement, is inspired by the work of Gunther Kress and Theo van Leeuwen and the compositional framework they set forth in *Reading Images: The Grammar of Visual Design*, as well as by Emilia Djonov and Theo van Leeuwen's study of layout as a meaning-making resource in "Between the Grid and Composition: Layout in PowerPoint's Design and Use." The ideas in those works are integrated here with the functional and accessible affordances of presentation software to help you apply them in your everyday slide designs.

10.1

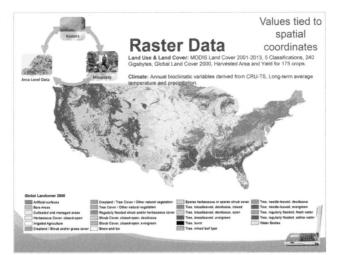

10.2

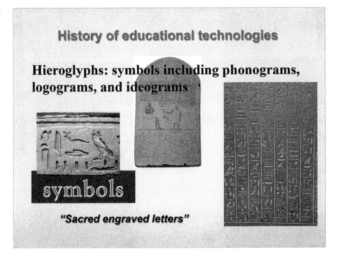

10.3

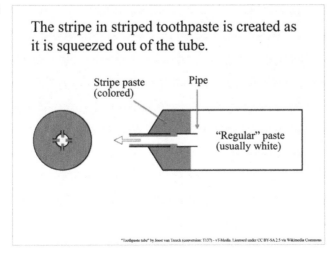

These composition problems make it harder for students to figure out what the slide is telling them, which in turn means it will take them longer to return their attention to you. You'll need to learn to recognize and assess the overall effect of your designs so you can identify and correct these types of mistakes as they occur in your compositions.

The good news is that all these problems can be fixed through awareness and intentionality.

Use Predefined Layouts to Add Content to Slides

You can solve many composition issues by using your presentation software's layouts.

Layouts are comprised of content placeholders, into which you can drop title text, body text, or graphics. Placeholders aren't the same as the text boxes that you manually create using the text box tool; instead, they're content containers with unique properties that tell the software how to display the information you put into them. Placeholders can only be altered from within the Slide Master.

All the major slideware applications include a selection of layouts. Figure 10.4 shows the default layout options available in PowerPoint.

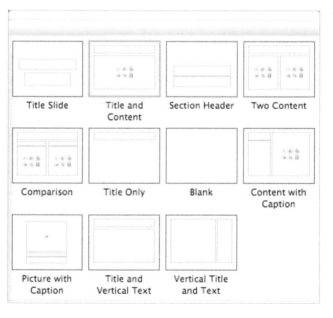

10.4

Layouts Create Structure

You should use layouts instead of manually created text boxes for a number of reasons. First, layouts create a subtle, consistent structure that helps students orient themselves from slide to slide. For example, the title is always at the top, and slide numbers are in a consistent spot somewhere along the bottom. Layouts also help students with wayfinding; section header slides look distinct from other layouts and are therefore instantly distinguished from content slides. Consistency helps students "learn" your slides, which means they'll come to be able to predict how you usually handle image citations, references, and so on.

Layouts Ensure a Point of Entry

Layouts can help ensure a predictable pattern that helps students move through the slide design. We naturally want to follow a Z-shape pattern as we look at a slide, as simulated in Figure 10.5. This natural tendency provides a compelling reason to make sure that most of your slides contain brief, descriptive text in the top left corner.

10.5

Consider again more closely the composition problem in Figure 10.1. The problem with this design is that it's not clear where to look first. The graphic that occupies the center is biggest so it catches the eye first, but it looks complex, and your students will want some help to interpret what it says. They'll look below and find an equally complex legend. In looking for more clues, they'll move up to the top left corner but will find two unhelpful elements there: a logo and a website. Moving along the top of the slide, following the natural Z pattern, they'll find three lines of tiny text and a piece of clip art. After a lot of searching, it's still difficult to discern the point of this slide. Let's redo this one using the predefined title-plus-content layout (Figure 10.6).

Much better. A smooth entry into the design means students will get in, get the point, and get their attention back to you as quickly as possible.

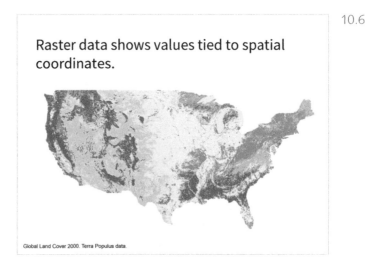

10.6

Raster data shows values tied to spatial coordinates.

Global Land Cover 2000. Terra Populus data.

Layouts Improve Workflows

Using predefined layouts not only results in a more consistent, predictable visual structure, but they can make your life easier as well. Should you want to change the font for every slide in the deck, you can make the formatting change to the placeholder in the Slide Master, which automatically makes the change for every slide in the deck.

Layouts "Speak" to Other Applications

For advanced users and instructional designers, predefined layouts govern additional functionality outside the slides themselves. For example, placeholder text can make converting a slide presentation into an eLearning module easier. Text captured in the title placeholders will be imported as table of contents entries in eLearning authoring applications like Adobe Captivate or Articulate Storyline. When each slide has a unique title, it also helps create a navigational mechanism in web-embedded Google Slides presentations that can act like a table of contents, as shown in the bottom left corner of Figure 10.7.

10.7

Layouts Are More Accessible

Last, screen readers can more easily access the information entered into predefined layouts, though, as I've said, distributing the slide file itself isn't the main recommendation of this book (see Lesson 4).

Control Visual Hierarchy

Visual hierarchy refers to the order in which the eye notices and attends to individual elements in a design; we're wired to notice things that are big, bold, bright, or in motion. You can control the visual hierarchy of your slides by leveraging the biology of visual perception, but first you need to decide what elements should be made bigger, bolder, or brighter. Here is an intersection between design and information: Generally, you'll want to draw students' attention to the most important information first—make that the focal point, the most attention-getting part of the design. Then visually downplay subordinate information by making those elements smaller, less bold, and less bright. This is another reason among many why you must be intentional in articulating the communication goal of each and every slide.

Look again more closely at Figure 10.2. The chief problem with having this many different images and in this arrangement is that there is neither a clear point of entry nor an obvious path around the slide. Recall that pretty and functional designs are simple, clear, and consistent, and slides that lack a clear point of entry or predictable eye path won't be perceived in these ways.

Typically the easiest way to control hierarchy is to make the most important item the biggest, boldest, most saturated, or brightest. You only need one of these techniques to get the job done. In the makeover (Figure 10.8), I identified the main point of the slide—that hieroglyphs are symbols that may be phonogram, logogram, or ideogram. The main content idea helped inform the design decision to show the context of a group of hieroglyphs, zooming in on a few of them for closer examination. I made the "zoom" the focal point by making it biggest. The important thing is that it's clear which thing to look at first; it isn't necessary to get bogged down with guessing what students will look at second, third, and fourth.

In this and in every makeover presented in this book, there is a clear path for the eye to follow that correlates with the content.

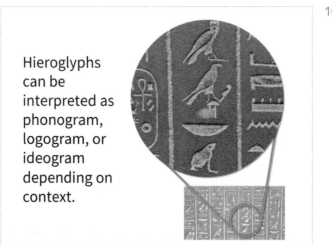

10.8

Hieroglyphs can be interpreted as phonogram, logogram, or ideogram depending on context.

Information Value in Composition

Consider what you already know about the design in Figure 10.9, even if you don't know what the words mean. When you put a large object in the center of a slide, you're communicating not only the importance of that thing but also the relative lesser importance of other items arranged around it. This principle can help you organize content when you have a number of items to arrange on the slide.

Placement of elements on the slide canvas can influence students' understanding of the meaning of the information, even if subtly, and even if they aren't necessarily able to articulate it.

10.9

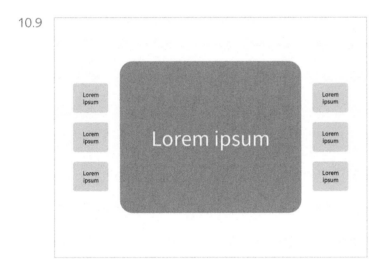

What Layouts to Use?

A basic set of five layouts is adequate for most academic slide design tasks: Title Slide, Title Only, Blank, Section Header, and Emphasis. The Emphasis layout is a blank slide with one placeholder for large text, useful for text-based treatments (Lesson 5) or section headers. Google Slides has a similar layout called Main Point that can be used as Emphasis. If you're using PowerPoint, Keynote, or LibreOffice Impress, you'll need to build this one as a custom layout using the Slide Master.

The Title and Content layout has previously been implicated in the essential inefficacy of traditional topic-subtopic slide designs, though each layout has its uses where you have a well-articulated reason to use bullet points (see Lesson 14). The Title and Two Content layout can be useful where you plan to make meaningful use of left-right polarization in your composition.

Left and Right

Western audiences assign special meaning to objects arranged left to right. Juxtaposing two items sets up an expectation of comparison between two states or two conditions. Because we perceive the start of things to be on the left and forward motion to proceed rightward, we therefore expect the "before" to be on the left and the "after" to be on the right. Likewise, we expect the "cause" to be on the left and the "effect" to be on the right.

Furthermore, we expect to see "pros" on the left and "cons" on the right (see Figure 14.7). Recall the third composition problem slide, Figure 10.3, which shows how toothpaste gets its stripe. It uses a left-right composition but violates the tacit understanding of the meaning of items positioned on left (before) and right (after), as well as forward movement in time, which is expected to move from left to right. The makeover (Figure 10.10) corrects these issues by flipping the graphic so the squeeze (beginning) happens left and the emergence of the paste (end) happens right. I also move the entire tube to the left and offset the size and positioning of the front of the tube, labeling both views so students can tell at a glance what they're looking at. The result is a graphic that more clearly communicates this message.

To violate any of these expectations may add layers of confusion, subtle or not.

10.10

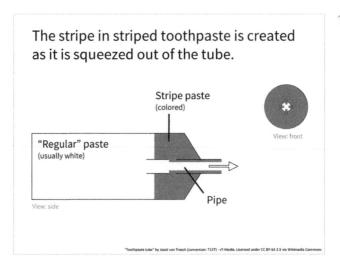

The Vertical Timeline: A Makeover

Western audiences assign special meaning to objects arranged left to right. Researchers have noted that children across cultures automatically order things forward or backward in time according to a horizontal structure.* Let's compare two slides with the same information about the history of Zeppelin rigid airships. The first uses bullet points in a typical fashion (Figure 10.11). The second presents the same information as a horizontal timeline. The timeline version is more pleasing to the eye as well as easier to enter and to comprehend (Figure 10.12). One main reason is that the sequence of events is depicted

* From *The Cognitive Science of Visual-Spatial Displays: Implications for Design* by Mary Hegarty.

10.11

10.12

through the arrangement of the information on the slide, whereas the bulleted list relies on the viewer to mentally order and arrange the information going forward in time, which takes more cognitive resources.

Of course, it's not possible to provide examples of each of the types of visuospatial relationships that may crop up in your content. In the next lesson, we'll examine some other elements that can be leveraged for communicative purposes.

Exercises

1. Empowerment through custom layouts. The key to creating your own layouts is to work from within the Slide Master, using the slideware application's special placeholder fields—rather than manually created text boxes—to create "containers" for the content. If you don't know how to access your slideware application's Slide Master or how to add placeholder fields to a master slide, you can easily find video tutorials via an internet search. After you've constructed it, give your new layout a name and save it. Close the Slide Master and return to the application's design area. Create a new slide using the layout you created, noticing how the layout works to control the visual appearance and positioning of slide content.

2. Composition scout. Do an internet image search for midcentury advertisements like appliances, cosmetics, furniture, or cars. This time you're looking more at the images than the text. Pay attention to the placement of the products in the ads. What patterns do you see? When the product is central, what elements are placed in the margins? Chances are you'll see that central images are big and bold. The designer wanted you to notice the promoted product first and to perceive the competition as little, small, subordinate, inferior.

By the same token, when you see a left-right polar arrangement, what state or condition is depicted on the left versus the right? Chances are you'll always find a before-and-after condition depicted left to right. These embedded meanings have their roots in ancient art and still subtly influence our experience of graphic designs today; consider how you can use these techniques to make your own designs more effective and efficient.

Effective Use of Color
for Teaching and Learning

*Color is a huge topic that can be approached from the physiological
(the rods and cones in our eyeballs that help us perceive color) or the physical
(the wavelengths that comprise the color spectrum). However, the discussion
in this lesson comes at the topic from a purely practical standpoint: how to use color
effectively for teaching and learning. We'll first discuss the reasons to stick with
a limited palette of colors throughout the design process. Next, we'll talk about the
role of color in communication, specifically, how you can use it for functional rather
than decorative purposes. We'll also discuss ways to avoid some common color
combination pitfalls. At the end of this lesson, you'll know enough about
color to make strong, intentional choices in your designs.*

Color Conveys Meaning

Color is a powerful communication tool. Whether we're aware of it or
not, we expect color to carry information. Therefore, when we see a
display like Figure 11.1, we expect there to be some reason that the
theme block is colored differently than other blocks of similar shape
and size. Students will always try to figure out the reason for differences on a slide. If the content doesn't supply a reason, they will spend
some amount of mental effort making one up, and it may not be what
you intended. Therefore, you should be intentional about its use.

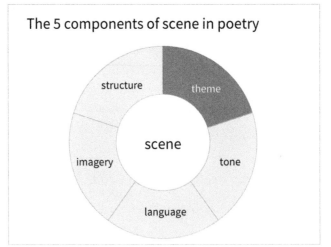

Reserve Color for Communication, Not Decoration

Color should always be functional rather than decorative. Figure 11.2 provides an example. The colors are decorative because they don't correlate with the scheme of the rest of the deck nor codify aspects of the Herbart method in future slides. Furthermore, they don't help differentiate the steps because that work is accomplished by the shapes and their arrangement. This instructor merely wanted to create a rainbow effect, presumably because they thought it looked nice. But the design is distracting; students will wonder what the significance of the colors are and whether they need to remember which color belongs with which step. Some students also may wonder whether this slide is attempting to make a political statement because the rainbow palette has long been culturally associated with gay pride.

Some Ideas That Can Be Communicated Using Color

What are some effective uses of color? Use it to call attention to a significant aspect of the design (Figure 11.3). Use it to show amount, quantity, or severity (Figure 11.4; notice that the darkest color is reserved for the largest or most, while the lightest color is for the smallest or least). Use color to show change or progression over time. Use it to differentiate sections in a graph. Or use it to provide a visual

11.2

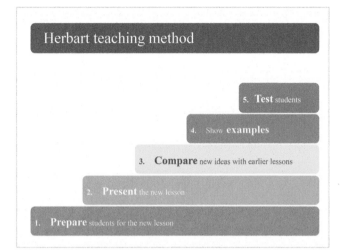

11.3

11.4

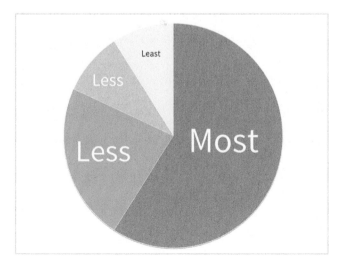

break in the action. For example, Figure 11.5 depicts a series of four slides where the guidepost (section header) slide indicates the start of a new topic, providing a visual change of pace without breaking the cohesion of the deck as a whole.

You also can use color to guide attention, which we'll discuss in Lesson 13.

Color can be overwhelming otherwise, and a slide deck can quickly start to look incohesive. To make successful color decisions, you'll need to establish a plan. In the next section, we'll discuss how to create a color system.

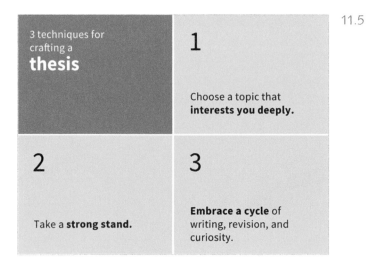

11.5

Why You Need a Color System

Throughout the book, I've talked about consistency, clarity, and simplicity as guiding principles that can help you make more intentional design decisions from slide to slide. Taken together, individual slide decisions contribute toward a cohesive deck. Choosing a set of colors is a significant decision because it can directly impact the cohesiveness of your deck. For this reason, I suggest making it simple for yourself by following this basic rule: Choose just four colors and stick with them for every slide in the deck.

Most everyday slide design tasks require the use of only four highly contrasting colors. Far from limiting your creativity, you'll make life easier for both yourself and your students if you follow this advice.

First, you're making your slides more functional for students who have low vision or low visual literacy or who simply happen to be sitting farthest away from the projector. Second, you're freeing up more of their cognitive resources because they'll only have to figure out your system once, at the beginning of the presentation. They won't need to decode "what color means what" on each individual slide. Finally, your slide decks will look instantly more unified and therefore more professional.

At the same time, you make your own life easier. Deciding on one set of colors for the whole design process means you won't have to make the same decision ("What color to use?") twenty or fifty times, for however many slides are in your deck. As a result, you'll have more control over your instructional messages, instead of letting the software make the decisions for you and arbitrarily adding colors that may or may not communicate the meaning or style you intend.

Last, having a color system rescues you and your students from the bidirectional perils of color-coding.

Never Make Students Decode Your Color-Coding

Color-coding always seems like a good idea at first. You think to yourself: *I'm going to use blue to indicate* this *and green to indicate* that. Two weeks later, you return to the project and have to figure out your own color-coding system again before you can even get back to the design task. It's a waste of time even in your own personal workflows, and even more so for anyone you might subject to look at them. The reason is because color choices are often arbitrary, and you usually need a legend or key to make sense of them later.

Your color system shouldn't be so complex that students need to decode it in order to use it. It's a system because it's meant to help you make consistent decisions and to use color for information-carrying purposes rather than as decoration, which is why it's liberating to use just four colors.

If you ever do need to color-code something, such as a bar chart with multiple variables, make sure the legend appears prominently on the slide. If a color code is necessary to interpret information that appears across several slides, include the legend on each of those slides. In these ways, you reduce the amount of effort students will spend decoding your visuals so they can spend more time focused on content.

Create a Color System

Intentionality transforms a color palette into a functional system, one that uses color to help communicate the instructional message, rather than decorate it. To this end, each color should have a specified primary use. Choose

- one solid color for text,

- one for background, and

- two for showing emphasis.

The text and background colors should be neutral and unobtrusive. For the emphasis colors, choose a "pop" color that's brighter, and a secondary emphasis color that contrasts well against the others but is richer rather than brighter than the pop color. These are *primary* intended uses, not to be held hard and fast. You should feel free to switch things up where there is a functional reason to do so.

Next, you'll need to make sure your colors have strong contrast.

Use Strong Color Contrast

All students benefit from your use of strong contrast between colors, and students should never have to struggle to discriminate two different colors on your slides. What does it mean to have strong contrast? Consider the differences between the blocks in Figure 11.6. The blocks on the left are more difficult to distinguish than the ones on the right because the two shades of blue on the left have poor contrast.

Contrast is about differences in brightness and darkness. When you put one color on top of another, choose one that is very bright and one that is very dark. The highest possible contrast is black on white or white on black, though you needn't limit yourself to those colors. To really get a sense of whether your color system is accessible, you'll need to check them against each other in all possible combinations. The internet has lots of tools to help.

11.6

Use a Color Accessibility Checker to Test Contrast

Here I've selected a system of four colors to test (Figure 11.7): light gray for text, black for background, magenta as the pop color, and gold as a secondary emphasis color. I picked these colors based on a guess, knowing that very bright things create strong contrast against very dark things.

An online color contrast checker helps me determine which combinations of these colors are accessible, that is, whether they have adequate contrast when displayed one on top of the other. A palette of four colors will never be entirely accessible in all of its twelve possible combinations, but the tool can help determine which combinations do work. Next, I'll need the computer color codes, or hexadecimal values, that correspond to each of the four colors in order to test them for adequate contrast.

11.7

Find the Hexadecimal Values

All colors that are represented in digital environments have associated number-and-letter values, which computers use to determine how to display them. These codes are called *hexadecimal* or *hex values*. The hex values associated with the swatches in Figure 11.7 are light gray: #f2f2f2; magenta: #ff00ff; gold: #faa414; and black: #000000.

PowerPoint gives color values in a different notation, called *RGB values*, which indicate the amounts of red, green, and blue (RGB) in each hue. (Hex values also tell the amounts of each of red, green, and blue; the notation means #RRGGBB.) Where you know the RGB values of the colors you want to test, you can use an online converter tool to find the hex values.

Aside from checking color contrast, it's useful to know the RGB and hex values of your preferred colors. If you want to use them in two different places—for example, to use the same palette in your course website that you use in your PowerPoint presentations—these values can help you recreate the exact hues in both spots.

If all this sounds complicated, don't worry. You can access accessible palettes and suggested uses for each hue in the palette at z.umn.edu/accessiblecolor.

Want to learn more? Keep reading!

Lots of accessibility checkers are available online, but I like the one from North Carolina State University (at https://accessibility.oit.ncsu.edu/tools/color-contrast/) because it allows you to check multiple combinations at once. Here is where I need to have either the RGB or hex values for each of my colors, because I'll enter this information into the tool. I'm interested in the results of the test of 18-point font or greater, because the size of text I'll typically use on my slides will be bigger than 18 points.

Figure 11.8 shows the results of the contrast check. Although this color system passes with magenta on black and black on magenta (as indicated in column 4, "Pass or Fail"), it fails in other combinations: magenta on gold, gold on magenta, magenta on gray, and gray on magenta.

From this information, I know that I shouldn't use combinations of gold on magenta or even gray on magenta. The use of this palette in Figure 11.9, for example, is inaccessible (and, some of my friends have argued, a bit "garish early '90s").

However, this same set of colors *does* pass on all possible combinations where either the light gray or the black is the background (Figure 11.10).

11.8

Large Non-Bold Text (18pt or greater, or approximately 1.5em rendered) for FF4BFC

Color Code	Sample Text	Sample Text (inverted)	Pass or Fail	Ratio (pass>=3.0)
F5F5F5	Lorem ipsum	Lorem ipsum	FAIL	2.51
FBB131	Lorem ipsum	Lorem ipsum	FAIL	1.49
000000	Lorem ipsum	Lorem ipsum	PASS	7.66

11.9

11.10

Large Non-Bold Text (18pt or greater, or approximately 1.5em rendered) for 000000

Color Code	Sample Text	Sample Text (inverted)	Pass or Fail	Ratio (pass>=3.0)
F5F5F5	Lorem ipsum	Lorem ipsum	PASS	19.26
FF4BFC	Lorem ipsum	Lorem ipsum	PASS	7.66
FBB131	Lorem ipsum	Lorem ipsum	PASS	11.44

Based on this information, I could successfully combine these colors as depicted in Figure 11.11.

Some lessons we can draw from these tests:

1. Creating accessible color palettes is actually somewhat challenging. It's even harder when the background isn't a solid color.

2. Accessibility is context- and content-dependent, and no one-size-fits-all set of colors will work well in every situation.

3. It's best to stick with a very bright color against a very dark background or vice versa.

11.11

Use a Combination of Cues to Differentiate Information with Color

To reiterate an important point, color should never be the sole means for communicating information, because some students won't be able to perceive the information carried by the colors.

In the graph at the top of Figure 11.12, the contrast between the two colors used to distinguish protein from fat counts is inadequate. You can easily fix the problem by adding a pattern to the display area of the fat variable (as shown in the bottom slide).

To create text emphasis using color, combine boldface text along with the differentiated color, or bold and a colored highlight box in the background. Lesson 13 offers additional ways to make text stand out on your slides.

11.12

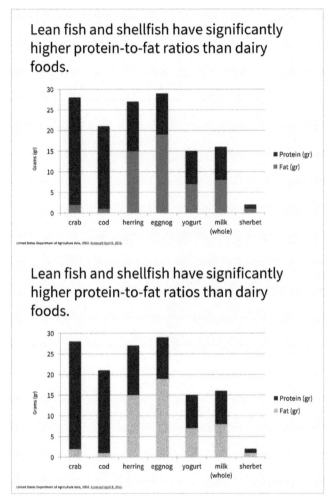

Color Vibrations Aren't Good Vibrations

Sometimes colors that have similar properties vibrate (or conflict) when juxtaposed or placed one on top of the other. Beyond just being an unnecessary distraction, color vibration can actually have a physically adverse effect on students. This is another reason to test all combinations of your color system against each other to make sure they don't vibrate. You can tell if the colors in your chosen color system vibrate by placing text from one color on top of a larger area of the other color. The typical offenders are bright orange and bright blue and bright red and bright green (Figure 11.13). Even just changing the tint (lightness) or shade (darkness) of one of the two colors can mitigate the vibration.

11.13

Color Gradients

Color gradients often are used to create depth or visual interest inside an enclosed space and, indeed, are part of the default styling of many of the themes and shapes in PowerPoint and Keynote. However, gradients can quickly make slides unreadable. Compare the two shapes in Figure 11.14 and note how the text in the gradient shape starts to disappear as you read from left to right, due to the decreasing contrast between text and background color. The text in the bottom shape is much easier to read because it's a solid text color against a solid background. Clearly, you should avoid color gradients wherever possible because they're difficult to design around. You have more important things to do.

11.14

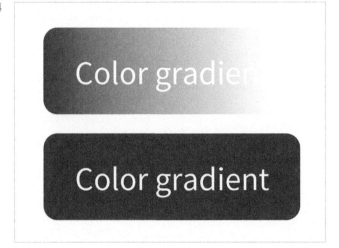

Exercises

1. Apply a predetermined color palette. The color palettes in your slideware likely are tied to the design themes, though PowerPoint and Google Slides both allow you to decouple theme from palette. Take one of your existing decks and apply several of the different palettes to it, one at a time, noticing the way the software applies the palette to text and shapes. Which colors create emphasis within, for example, charts or other data displays? What color indicates a hyperlink? Do you agree with the default color applications? Do the colors have enough contrast between them? If not, find the controls within your slideware that allow you to change how color is used. Get to know what's possible in terms of overriding the default color choices in your slideware.

2. RGB and hexadecimal values. Learn where to find the RGB and hexadecimal values in your presentation software. This knowledge can empower you to figure out how to use your favorite colors across applications and contexts, web- and desktop-based.

3. Create your own color system. Your slideware includes a number of preset color palettes, each of which includes more colors than needed for most design tasks (though they're useful in the creation of charts and graphs). The difference between a color palette and a color system is defining how you intend to use each color in the palette, so in this exercise, you'll define your own system by identifying not only the colors but also their primary use. You'll also make sure the system is accessible, that is, that the colors offer strong contrast when displayed next to one another.

a. Select a set of four colors. Specify a primary use for each: background, body text, primary emphasis, and secondary emphasis. Use an online tool or your slideware application to find the hexadecimal and RGB values.

b. Create a sample slide using the four colors in your system. Take a picture of the slide (save it as a jpeg or png file on your computer) and upload it to a color blindness simulator so you can see what it would look like to a student with any of the different types of color blindness.

c. Enter the hexadecimal or RGB values into an online color-contrast checker. Which combinations passed and which failed?

d. Adjust your color system based on pass/fail, and test again until you have a set that passes all marks. You now have a color system to use for your next slide deck.

4. Color evaluation. Now that you have a color system as well as a new understanding of the purpose of color in a slide deck, open one of your older decks and see what you notice about your old color ways. What colors did you used to be drawn to? How did you use them? Find some places in your old designs that used color as decoration and replace the decorative color with functional color. How did you do it? Did the design improve drastically, or was the change subtler? Chances are you'll have discovered another tool (color!) you can use to communicate intentionally and effectively.

Effective Typography
for Teaching and Learning

The number one question you're probably asking is: Which font should I use on my slides? A quick and easy answer—if you don't care to explore the topic further—is Verdana or Georgia. No matter which you choose, they both are good fonts, and they both come standard on modern computers and mobile devices. However, like most things in life, a true, one-size-fits-all answer is probably impossible. A closer examination of typography's complexities will help you make more informed decisions about how you display text on slides. Key to both practical and professional-level typography is always this: Typography is successful when your audience doesn't notice it. *This condition is called* transparent typography. *In this lesson we'll talk about ways to achieve transparent typography as well as practical decisions you'll need to make in solving common typographical problems. At the core of this lesson are a lot of don'ts: Don't center text. Don't use all caps. Don't underline. Don't bold (excessively). Don't italicize. Don't mix fonts. If you're balking right now at what feels like an unnecessarily lengthy set of constraints, I hope that by the end you'll actually find them more of a relief than a constraint.*

Choose One Font for the Entire Deck

Choose one font and use it consistently throughout the whole deck. The reasons for this recommendation are many. Most notably, humans naturally look for patterns in incoming information and try to ascribe

* To be precise, a *font* is the file that lives on your computer that tells the computer how to draw the text. A *typeface* is the technical name for the collection of designed letterforms. However, I'll talk fonts instead of typefaces, because most people who aren't graphic designers use the terms interchangeably.

meaning to the differences in these established patterns. Notice the mixing of fonts[*] that's going on in Figure 12.1.

Some segment of this instructor's students are going to be distracted by the differences in fonts, wondering whether those differences have some significance, such as varying levels of importance. Of course, the truth is probably just that its creator was cutting and pasting from several sources and forgot to change the fonts to the same one when they were finished (which would bug the perfectionists in the class). Either way, lack of font unity has caused an unnecessary distraction, and the effect can make the instructor seem careless or unprofessional.

12.1

Vestal virgins

- In ancient Roman religion, the Vestals or Vestal Virgins were priestesses of Vesta, goddess of the hearth.
- The Vestals became powerful and influential in the Roman state, held in awe, and attributed certain magical powers.
- The Vestals were committed to the priesthood before puberty (6–10 years old) and sworn to celibacy for 30 years.
- Once retired, a former Vestal was given a pension and allowed to marry.
- To obtain entry into the order, a girl had to be free of physical and mental defects, have two living parents and be a daughter of a free-born resident of Rome.
- The punishment for violating the oath of celibacy was to be buried alive.

A second reason to choose a consistent font is for that segment of your students who have cognitive disabilities like dyslexia. Dyslexia already makes it difficult for those students to read on-screen text, and mixing fonts can create an even greater challenge.

Third, font mixing is difficult to do well without looking amateurish. Fonts are difficult to mix because the shapes of the individual letters, as well as the conveyed emotion (more on that in a minute), don't always mesh well when juxtaposed. Graphic designers study typography extensively to learn this complex skill.

You may protest that you need at least a couple of fonts to emphasize important material. I agree that a contrasting type style can help create emphasis. The good news is that you can instead select a few members of the same font family. Most quality fonts come with a number of font weights in what is known as its family. You can achieve different emphasis through contrast and still have a cohesive-looking deck by mixing font weights. The regular, everyday fonts in your slideware application, like Times New Roman and Arial, also have a bold, an italic, and sometimes also a bold italic. Typefaces purchased from font foundries for commercial graphic design work often have even more weights to choose from; Figure 12.2 showcases the beautiful Avenir with six other members of its family.

However, you don't need to go out and purchase high-end fonts; for everyday communication you can effectively leverage the ones that come already installed on your computer. The point is that using several weights of the same font means they'll always look good together. Because they're based on the same letter shapes, they will look cohesive yet distinct when they're used in close proximity.

12.2

Choose 1 typeface with multiple weights.

Avenir Book
Avenir Book Oblique
Avenir Book Roman
Avenir Black
Avenir Light
Avenir Medium
Avenir Heavy

Choose a Plain Typeface
Rather Than a Display Typeface

Known as body text fonts in graphic design, plain fonts are best for teaching slides. First, they're easy to read because the individual letter shapes that comprise them are uniform and predictable. Look at the smooth, predictable shapes of the letters that comprise each of the plain fonts in Figure 12.3.

Body text fonts should be distinguished from display or decorative fonts, which are typically used to apply a specific tone or style to a

Helvetica

Calibri

Times New Roman

Garamond

design. Notice the stylized shapes and flourishes in the letterforms that comprise the display fonts in Figure 12.4.

Of course, the flourishes and irregularities are what make display fonts so useful for conveying style and emotion in professionally designed pieces. In fact, you can spot a display font by the feel (emotion or tone) it creates. However, besides conveying a distinct emotional tone that is quite likely inappropriate to an academic presentation, display fonts are harder to read than plain fonts and can pose legibility problems for students.

Bilbo Swash Caps

Bauhaus 93

Comic Sans

Life Savers

In addition to legibility and readability, another advantage of choosing plain fonts (Calibri, Times New Roman, Helvetica, Arial, and the like) is that they're likely to be already installed on any computer. If you compose your whole deck using the LifeSavers font (shown in Figure 12.4) on your own computer and go to present your lecture on the computer in a lecture hall or someone else's classroom, the computer will search for LifeSavers and, not finding the font file, will substitute a different one, which could destroy your careful formatting. (This is a hazard only when you're using desktop-based software like PowerPoint, Keynote, or LibreOffice Impress. Google Slides are stored in the cloud, so the fonts you use in them will always be available.)

I hope you're convinced by now that it's best to pick one plain font for your deck. It's the smooth, predictable shapes of the individual letters in those tried and true, plain fonts that make them transparent (i.e., easy to read and emotionally neutral) and therefore the best choice for teaching and learning contexts.

That brings us to the next logical question: Which font family should you use?

Which Font Family to Use?

As I mentioned in the introduction to this chapter, a solid, quick answer to this question is to use Verdana, if you like a sans serif font, or Georgia, if your preference is for serifs.

Serifs are the little "caps" that appear on the terminal points of letters. Common serif fonts are Times New Roman and Garamond. Sans serif fonts, like Arial and Helvetica, don't have these caps (*sans* means without). You may have heard that you should choose sans serif fonts for slide presentations. This advice was the rule twenty or thirty years ago when screen resolutions for desktop computers and laptops were poor, making it difficult for audiences to decipher the serifs on the ends of the letters. These days, screen resolutions are crisp and clear, and you should generally feel free to select whatever body text font you like best, serif or sans.

Both Verdana and Georgia are body text fonts that were developed to be read on screens. Both come in the four weights I mentioned previously: regular, italic, bold, and bold italic. Both are essentially transparent in that they don't evoke noticeable emotion on their own. However, some evidence suggests that sans serif fonts are easier to read for people who have dyslexia and for people who are reading from mobile devices with small screens. Given these two use cases, Verdana might win out over Georgia, but other plain, sans serif fonts can work as well.

Techniques for Typographical Emphasis

Text has two functions on a slide: to tell the message and to show what's most important within the message. This section takes a closer look at how to visually indicate important information. The rule is: Never rely on color alone or font weight alone to show emphasis.

Students with visual impairments will have trouble distinguishing between colors, and they may miss the emphasis all together. The best way to create emphasis in a line of text is to use a combination of contrasting font weight and color, as in Figure 12.5.

The worst techniques to use for typographical emphasis are to underline, italicize, or use drop shadows, text outlining, or any of the other nonstandard text-formatting options that slideware offers.

12.5

Driver characters in film and fiction
and their archetypal equivalents

Protagonist
Hero

Antagonist
Shadow

Guardian
Mentor

Contagonist
Trickster

Don't Underline

In the digital age, underlined text is assumed to be a hyperlink. For this reason, reserve underlining for those times when you're actually displaying a hyperlink. Underlined text that doesn't lead anywhere online when clicked will just look like a mistake—a broken link.

Don't Italicize

Italics are difficult to read, especially in large quantities and especially for students with any kind of reading difficulty. Italics also can be confused with other semantic connotations, such as foreign language words or taxonomical classifications (e.g., *Homo sapiens*). Some academic style guides, such as the Modern Language Association (MLA), dictate that book titles should be italicized. Reserve italics for those specific situations rather than as a means of emphasizing important material.

Don't Use Drop Shadows, Text Outlines, or Other Nonstandard Text Formatting

Drop shadows (like the text in Figure 12.6), text outlines, and other nonstandard text formatting can interfere with text legibility, which is especially true of on-screen text. Transparent typography isn't happening if your students have to strain to read the words on the slide.

The slide shown in Figure 12.6 attempts to contrast the definitions of socialism with Marxism and communism.

12.6

You and I have been together for a while now, so I know you can easily point out all of the reasons this slide is ineffective, but let's go ahead and list them anyway. From a content standpoint, this slide contains too many ideas. Spatially, the slide has too much text and not enough white space. From a color perspective, the gradient in the background makes the text appear bright white at the top and fade to gray toward the bottom, creating an unwelcome text-scrolling effect reminiscent of the opening sequence from the *Star Wars* movies. From a typography perspective, the body text is more difficult to read than it should be because both a drop shadow and black outline have been applied to it. In addition, the underlining leads students to believe that the two headings are hyperlinks. You may ask yourself: *Where do those links go? Am I missing something if I don't get to click on them?*

In the makeover (Figure 12.7), I solve the content overload problems by removing one of the two definitions so that this slide has only one job to do, that is, to define socialism. I replace the colored gradient with a solid background. Then I use a combination of size and font weight contrasts to increase the text's effectiveness in communicating the definition. (I'll use a second slide to create the Marxism/communism definition slide.)

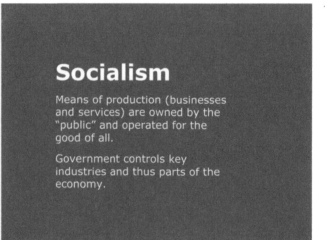

12.7

Use Strong Font Contrasts

Robin Williams says in her classic (and highly recommended), *The Non-Designer's Design Book*, "Contrast is not just for the aesthetic look of the piece. It is intrinsically tied in with the organization and clarity of the information on the page. Never forget that your point is to communicate." This is nowhere truer than in typographical emphasis. However, not all typefaces are created equal, and some have stronger contrasts of bold and regular weights than others. The Marxism/communism definition slide has been made over two ways in Figure 12.8. The top example uses the same Verdana typeface that was used in the socialism slide, but with a mix of 22-point and 28-point size and bold weight to emphasize the most important words. The bottom example does all the same things but with Adobe Caslon Pro.

The bold weight of Adobe Caslon Pro is more difficult to distinguish from its regular weight compared to the bold and regular weights of the Verdana. In many cases, students will miss important information all together if the contrast between two type styles is weak.

You can support the functional needs of students by creating strong contrasts of color, space, shape, and font size so they can more quickly perceive differences.

12.8

Strategic Bolding

Learning to use boldface type effectively can increase the efficacy of slides where your design necessarily is text heavy. Figure 12.9 represents the fewest words you could get away with on this preview slide about welding.

The austere treatment makes for a dull slide that gives too little information to be useful. Because it neglects to name the subject (welding), reading this slide becomes a little like deciphering a code. By contrast, the slide in Figure 12.10 essentializes the main points while retaining secondary, supporting information. It uses strategic bolding to focus learner attention on critical words.

12.9

In this talk we'll cover

1. Differences between traditional and laser
2. Definitions
3. Types
4. Basic process
5. Subtypes of processes
6. Advantages, limitations

12.10

In this talk we'll cover

1. **Differences** between traditional and laser welding
2. **Definition** of laser beams and laser basics
3. **Types** of lasers
4. Laser welding, basic **process**
5. **Subtypes** of laser welding processes: gas, disk YAG, and fiber
6. **Advantages** and **limitations**

Plain and simple, this talk is going to cover

- Differences
- Definitions
- Types
- Processes
- Subtypes
- Advantages and limitations

The critical words are both bolded and given a color highlight rather than using either technique alone.

By the same token, make sure that your bolding choices reflect student—rather than instructor—goals. The preview slide in Figure 12.11, taken from a lecture introducing the major periods of English literature, bolded the words that might be most important from the teacher's point of view. After all, the instructor's job is to teach toward demonstrable outcomes. Learning the content is the student's primary job. However, the typographical emphasis of this list forces the student to focus on the instructor's outcomes (list, recognize, explain, recognize, name) rather than on the

12.11

By the end of this talk, you will be able to

- **List** the main literary periods in English literature
- **Recognize** the historical setting of each period
- **Explain** the main characteristics of each period
- **Recognize** the development from one period to another
- **Name** the main writers in each period

content itself. Although the student ought to be made aware of desired outcomes, a more student-centric bolding job would look like Figure 12.12.

Now the student's scanning eye will focus on

- Main literary periods
- Historical settings
- Characteristics
- Developments from one period to another
- Main writers

12.12

By the end of this talk, you will be able to

- List the **main literary periods** in English literature

- Recognize the **historical settings** of each period

- Explain the main **characteristics** of each period

- Recognize the **developments from one period to another**

- Name the **main writers** in each period

Strategic, student-centered use of boldface type in this objectives slide will help students prepare and listen for the main content and, in this way, is more likely to have a positive impact on the instructor's desired goals for the lecture.

Left Justify Rather Than Center Text

Centered text makes for harder on-screen reading. Our eyes must do a carriage return to find the beginning of each new line (as simulated by the uneven line on the left in Figure 12.13).

By contrast, left justification makes it easier to read because our eyes can consistently return to the same place at the beginning of each new line (as simulated by the straight vertical line at left in Figure 12.14).* You should left justify in almost all cases but particularly in blocks of text that are more than one line long.

* This concept is borrowed from Linda Lohr's *Creating Graphics for Learning and Performance.*

12.13

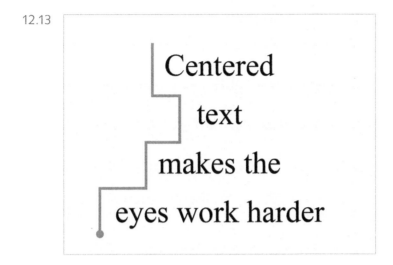

Centered text makes the eyes work harder

12.14

Left-justified text is easier on the eyes.

Don't Full-Justify Either

Justifying text is the typographical term for mathematically aligning both left and right edges of a paragraph of text. Although it's nice for books, it's never a good idea for on-screen reading. Justifying text inadvertently creates awkward, inconsistent gaps between words and sometimes also between letters (Figure 12.15). The gaps make it more difficult to read text on a projected screen.

12.15

Bacon ipsum

Bacon ipsum dolor amet consectetur tongue capicola, landjaeger id spare ribs excepteur. Pork ball tip laborum sunt cow laboris beef ribs. Jerky quis aliquip pork loin. Velit shank quis jerky in pancetta salami tri-tip incididunt pig ham adipisicing bacon aliqua it. Shank dolor non ba laborum sirloin.

Every seemingly minuscule decision you make in these matters is cumulative toward a transparent experience where students can be engaged with the lecture rather than struggling to read the slides.

Hyperlinks on Slides

You can display hyperlinks two ways on your slides. Either display the full text of the hyperlink (www.acadmicslidedesign.org) or embed the hyperlink in the text that describes what students will find when they follow it (Academic Slide Design). To decide which method to use, consider the context and what you want students to be able to do with the link. Displaying the full link text can look inelegant, but embedding the hyperlink within text means students can't copy it down (see Lesson 4).

A third method, a hybrid of these, exists that is useful when you want students to easily copy down the link. Asking them to copy down an unwieldy hyperlink (such as the kind generated by Google Docs: https://docs.google.com/1p2effmShbvXLKcB1MubCRjbwjG_Yeo4MnStr_iCtuII/slide=id.gb97b83273_0_32) is obviously impractical as well as inaccessible. Instead, you can use a URL shortener to create a shorter version that will be easier to copy down. URL-shortening services create a pointer that leads to where the real resource is located. The resulting hyperlink will still be a nonsensical string of numbers and letters, but shorter. Some services allow you to specify a string of human-readable text that would be easier to remember. Figure 12.16 displays a short link to chapter 7 notes as http://sho.rtURL/ch7notes.

An additional advantage of URL-shortening services is that they allow you to gather basic analytics, typically how many clicks your shortened URL received, which can be useful in gauging student engagement.

12.16

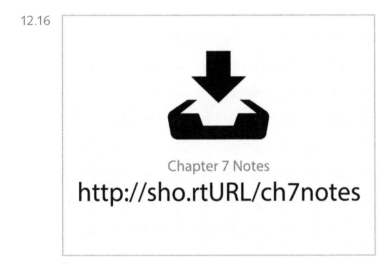

Chapter 7 Notes

http://sho.rtURL/ch7notes

Use Sentence Case, Not All Caps

ALL CAPS IS THIS. Sentence case is this. Title Case Is This.

Sentence case is best. The reason has to do with the way we read—which is actually by way of recognizing shapes rather than deciphering individual letters within each word. The net effect of a block of text in ALL CAPS is just that, a block (simulated by the red box around the letters in Figure 12.17).

12.17

CAPITAL LETTERS ARE HARDER TO READ

Your eye has to stop and recognize each individual letter in order to read it. Contrast with the experience of scanning a sentence that includes both upper and lowercase letters (simulated by the red outline of the letter shapes in Figure 12.18). The same advice applies to use of small caps: don't do it.

12.18

Because we actually read in patterns of expected shape combinations rather than letter by letter, we're able to read (scan) words written in sentence case much more quickly.

Title case is often found in the title, or heading, text box at the top of individual slides. In terms of readability, it's a better choice than all caps, but it still doesn't make sense following semantic guidelines for written English. Besides, because you've learned to use the assertion-evidence structure, you know that writing a short sentence in the title area at the top of the slide is actually a best practice; thus, title case is most appropriate only for the first slide in the deck and for mentions of book titles and other proper nouns.

Avoid WordArt

WordArt is a prebuilt gallery of graphical formatting options in PowerPoint that allows you to add decorative styling to text. LibreOffice Impress has a similar tool called Fontworks. Keynote offers a granular tool that does the same types of things but without the presets.

As Figure 12.19 illustrates, WordArt offers myriad options for altering the appearance of text: drop shadow (Oh no), reflection (Uff da), text outline (Yikes), glow (Woah, Nellie!), and bevel and emboss (Good grief). You may be seduced by the number of options. But these effects nearly all result in marginally legible atrocities. The options can be adjusted, so theoretically you ought to be able to customize a WordArt treatment to match the color and type system you've chosen for the rest of your deck; however, the options are difficult to control if you're trying to match the style of an existing design. Additionally, screen reader software can't reliably read WordArt, creating an accessibility issue. For these reasons, I recommend you avoid WordArt entirely. Your deck will look more professional if you do.

12.19

Control Line Spacing

Line spacing is the amount of white space between each line of text. The more lines of text you typeset, the more critical it is to know at least a little about the effect of line spacing and how it affects readability. Note the effect of too little space between the lines in Figure 12.20.

Scrunched together like this, it's difficult to distinguish the bottoms of the letters on one line from the tops of the letters on the next, and in one place the bottom of one letter even touches the top of another in the line below it (indicated by the highlight box). Remember, we don't read individual letters; we read by scanning for letter shapes, so the tops and bottoms of each line need breathing room. With too little space, our eyes have a harder time deciphering the shapes. These problems are compounded in large classrooms and conference halls where people are sitting far away from the projection screen.

12.20

Ipsum vegum

Turnip vulputate endive cauliflower in etit euismod kohlrabi. Amaranth sodales spinach ultrices velit. Avocado sem at daikon cabbage asparagus winter purslane erat kale. Celery ullamcorper potato scallion desert raisin horseradish spinach duis carrot in pulvinar mauris. Daikon erat cabbage asparagus winter purslane.

With too much line spacing, it's difficult to tell which lines belong together, a particular problem with bulleted information. In Figure 12.21, all the body text has been double-spaced. At first glance, it looks like there are seven distinct ideas here, because the seven lines are equidistant. On closer examination, though, you can see that the slide has only four ideas, as indicated by four bullet points. The line spacing creates a mismatch between the information and its display.

12.21

Ipsum vegum

• Turnip vulputate endive cauliflower in etit euismod

  kohlrabi

• Avocado sodales spinach ultrices velit.

• Amaranth sem at daikon cabbage asparagus winter

  purslane erat kale.

• Celery ullamcorper potato scallion desert raisin

  horseradish spinach duis carrot in pulvinar mauris.

In the makeover (Figure 12.22), the lines are single-spaced but with extra space added between each bullet point. Because lines that belong together are placed closer to each other (but not too close), it's easy to ascertain that there are four ideas on this slide.

You're probably thinking to yourself, *Why can't I just settle for the default amount of space that my slideware adds automatically?* Now that you've increased your visual literacy skills to this point, including an increased awareness of white space and balance and the effect of spatial positioning, you're going to start to notice a lot of defaults that could be improved. Empowerment is everything!

To this end, all four of the slideware applications referenced in the writing of this book (PowerPoint, Keynote, Google Slides, and LibreOffice Impress) allow a granular amount of control. Instead of using the single-, 1.5-, or 2.0- line-spacing presets, look for the setting that allows you to manually control the point size between each line. There is no hard-and-fast rule here, although an additional 6 or 8 points beyond the font size works well for the sizes that we're typically dealing with in slide design (e.g., 28-point and larger). Figure 12.22, the "just right" example, is set in 32-point text with line spacing at 18 points between each item. The 6-or-8-points-plus rule worked in my testing of fonts from 26 to 60 points and with a variety of body text fonts. To make sure you've done this right, you'll want to step back and look at your slides from the back of the room you'll be lecturing in. Note in the software how you can control the space before and after paragraphs and space between lines; you should learn to control both.

12.22

Ipsum **vegum**

- Turnip vulputate endive cauliflower in etit euismod kohlrabi.

- Amaranth sodales spinach ultrices velit.

- Avocado sem at daikon cabbage asparagus winter purslane erat kale.

- Celery ullamcorper potato scallion desert raisin horseradish spinach duis carrot in pulvinar mauris.

What you're after here is a happy medium: line spacing that makes it clear what belongs with what and also doesn't interfere with legibility or comprehension.

Exercises

1. Compare Times New Roman and Arial. Times New Roman and Arial are two fonts commonly installed on desktop computers, and they're both considered transparent fonts. While both are extremely readable, it's easy to tell the difference between them, both close up and from afar. Zoom in on the individual letters of each of these two fonts to compare and contrast them. What are the individual, physical differences that collectively make them look different? Hint: compare lowercase a's and g's, and capital Rs and Qs for key differences. The point of this exercise is to encourage you to look more closely at the features of the typography that's all around you.

2. Typography experiments. Open a slide deck for a talk that you've recently delivered. Highlight some of the text in a slide that contains a key message. Now take a moment to scroll through the list of fonts in your slideware. Change that text to Comic Sans. What is the effect on tone? Legibility? Try this now with some other fonts—something bold and brash like Braggadicio and something light and ephemeral like Josefin Sans. How does the perceived academic credibility of your content fare with each of these decisions? Finally, choose a font that you consider to be transparent and evaluate again. I hope this exercise helps convince you that body text fonts are the more appropriate choice for educational contexts.

3. Your toothpaste tube. Tonight as you're brushing your teeth, take a look at the toothpaste tube and the typefaces that appear on it, particularly the brand name. Is the brand name a serif or a sans serif font? Would you say that it's a display font or a plain font? It's quite likely that the text on the tube is trying to communicate to you the idea of pearly white teeth; identify some of the techniques, just in the words that are used on the tube, that communicate this idea to you.

4. Manual control. Copy and paste a short paragraph of text into a slide. Change it to 36-point font. Figure out how to manually set the line spacing at 44 points. Experiment with other point sizes so you get a feel for the effect of changing the amount of space. Contrast this more granular level of control with the typical spacing presets: 1.0, 1.5, and 2.0. Now see what happens when you repeat this exercise using a different font all together.

Techniques for Guiding Attention

Part of the skill of lecturing is maintaining students' attention over an extended period of time. Some of this work you'll accomplish using active lecturing techniques, and some can be helped along by visual design techniques. You can help students focus on what you're saying by using simple attention-guiding techniques that leverage the animation feature of your slideware application: progressive disclosure *(the oft-criticized but research-supported technique of concealing parts of your designs and then revealing them when you're ready to talk about them) and* annotation *(adding arrows or other shapes to call attention to certain areas of the screen). In this lesson you'll learn when and how to use these techniques, and soon you won't remember ever presenting without them.*

Guide Attention
Using Progressive Disclosure of Text

Use the animation feature of your slideware to reveal each piece of text on your slide only as you're ready to talk about it. This technique is called *progressive disclosure*, or *conceal and reveal*. With each reveal, you help renew and direct students' attention, and the information on the screen reinforces your verbal delivery. The visible information becomes manageable and digestible as opposed to a wall of words. Conceal and reveal helps students relax.

The animation functionality provides an overwhelming number of options: you can make a shape fly in or fly out at varying speeds, totter, gyrate, or rotate. Yet I hope you will disregard these options except for two: appear and disappear. Those other animation options are gimmicky and distracting. We're going for a subtle, gentle effect, not to add motion for motion's sake.

Animations, by the way, are distinct from slide transitions, which are the motion effects that you can insert in between slides. For example, you could have the content of one slide appear to "dissolve" in a checkerboard pattern as the next slide appears. Because movement is the most effective method for gaining attention, reserve it for that purpose; there's rarely a reason to add unnecessary movement in between slides—the change of content is enough. For these reasons, slide transitions are usually the motion-based equivalent of decoration in a live lecture situation. Avoid them unless you have a specific *content-related* reason to use them.

The following example is a full slide makeover that uses both animation and spatial positioning to communicate a key idea and supporting information, a synthesis of a number of techniques we've discussed. The original slide in Figure 13.1 is from a talk on the practice of human trafficking that poses the question of whether the term "people smuggling" is synonymous with the term "human trafficking."

You might remember that positioning the title at the bottom of the slide is ineffective because it disrupts the Z-shaped pattern that students' eyes follow as they read the slide. I'll take care of that issue first by moving the title text from the bottom to the top of the slide.

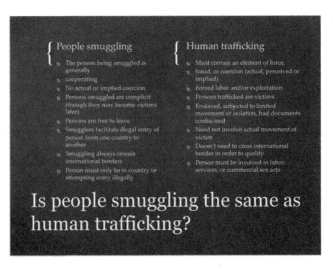

13.1

One effective aspect of the information in the original slide was the comparison between smuggling and trafficking. I want to retain this comparison in the new arrangement. But I also want to answer a logical question that students will have, which is, What are the distinguishing features of each of the terms, as well as the features they have in common? A Venn diagram is a natural choice to show where features are shared between two dissimilar things.

To populate the content of each circle, I select critical words from the sentence-like bullet points, creating some space between each item and making sure the analogs of each align left to right; for example, "Cooperation, consent" and "Force, fraud, or coercion" are direct comparisons between how people get smuggled and how they're trafficked. These items should be on the same line in order to facilitate the comparison.

I place the overlapping factors of each definition in the center of the Venn and add a contrasting color to emphasize the overlapping information, which contains the main idea—the features that smuggling and trafficking have in common (Figure 13.2).

The last step is to animate the display so that each of the direct comparisons can be made one at a time, revealing at the end where both concepts overlap. The series of screen captures in Figure 13.3 shows how the progressive disclosure would be presented to students as each point is discussed.

The progressive disclosure technique is versatile; you can use it for text, shapes, or a combination of both.

13.2

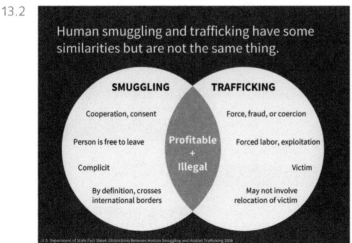

13.3

Guide Attention Using Color and Spatial Positioning

A second technique for guiding attention is to use a combination of color and spatial positioning. Figure 13.4 comes from a medical talk on a women's health issue, and it has some problems, most notably that there is no intentionality behind the color choices, no correlation between color and meaning. Shapes in the body of the slide are variously periwinkle, magenta, peach, white, and midnight blue. Both white and yellow text are used, all against a bright blue background.

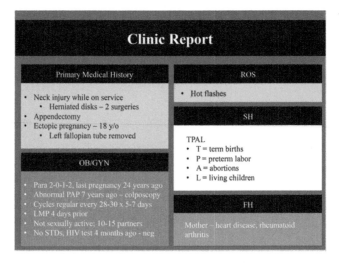

13.4

Within the deck this slide came from, different colors are used on different slides, confirming that color choice was haphazard.

The use of color in this design also is redundant, because the work of separating the information into categories has already been accomplished by the spatial arrangement of the boxes and the labels at the top of each box. However, the speaker wanted to keep all of this information on the same slide as a visual representation of the patient's medical history. This slide provides a perfect opportunity to show how color can help guide attention.

A makeover shows how color can be used more purposefully. As the lecturer talks through this slide, a gold background and darker text and title direct attention to the relevant parts of the design. Figure 13.5 shows multiple views of the slide where color highlights the section being discussed while the other sections are grayed out rather than hidden completely.

13.5

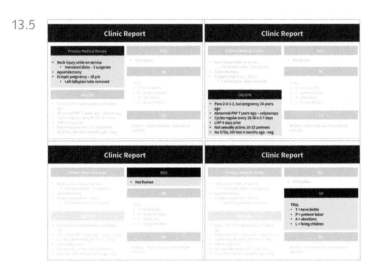

Guide Attention
Using Signaling Techniques

A third technique is to use signals like shapes, arrows, or lines to draw attention to the appropriate parts of the slide or graphic as you talk about each part. This technique is the on-screen equivalent of using a finger, stick, or laser pointer to draw attention to the section of interest.

The key to the success of this technique is to make sure the signal contrasts well against the background; otherwise students might miss it. Figure 13.6 shows both an unsuccessful (top) and successful (bottom) use of a colored box to draw attention to one part of this complex illustration, a lithograph of the historic Comstock Lode mining operation of the late 1800s in the United States.

13.6

Real-Time Annotation

In some of the more robust slideware applications, it is possible to use the annotation tools in real time while in Presentation mode. That is, you can mark up the slide as you're talking, using your mouse or trackpad. Some research says that students prefer real-time annotation to the type of preprogrammed techniques I've been talking about. Instructors may prefer it too; it allows them to respond to students' real-time inquiries. Key to the success of real-time annotation are—once again—ensuring a strong contrast between annotation and background and learning to narrate the annotations as you're doing them, to assist students who may have difficulty seeing or following along with the annotation.

Presenting Complex Structures

A challenging scenario for designers working on a 7.5- x 10-inch slide canvas is how to show a complex structure in its entirety before zooming in on any of its composite parts. You could divide the complete structure into pieces and show it in chunks across several slides, but that's not ideal because it segments what you're trying to show as a whole.

Prezi to the rescue!

Prezi's famous "infinite canvas" is unique among presentation software applications because it enables you to zoom in and out of a scene at varying levels of detail. Many people aren't fond of Prezi because they report that the motion and zooming makes them feel nauseated. But too much zoom and motion indicates either low skill (it's a hard tool to learn!) or misuse. Really, Prezi's biggest problem is that most presenters don't use it to its greatest advantage. If you're using Prezi to create the same old linear slides—view after view of bulleted lists—you're not leveraging Prezi's powerful potential.

Do use Prezi to help students see the bigger picture, the hierarchical structures, and the relationships that underlie complex content. For example, Figure 13.7 shows a workflow for collecting, processing, and analyzing data. This presenter could effectively use Prezi to show the entire workflow, zooming in to further explicate each part.

Do use Prezi to guide students through processes that have many interrelated steps or to put a long timeline in perspective. For example, Prezi would be a great tool to show the mind-boggling amount of time that biological organisms have been evolving on this planet and the mind-blowing amount of time the earth existed even before that.

Especially, do use Prezi to show an overarching organizational structure or visual metaphor. But don't be gimmicky. Reserve your Prezi energy for when it serves your subject matter—when seeing the overall organization of a topic really is the best way to make sense of it. Otherwise, be at peace with the fact that your content simply may not require Prezi's infinite canvas. When that's the case, use regular old slides, which are easier to master.

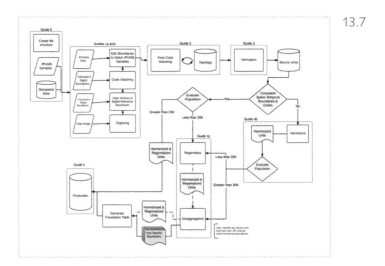

13.7

Exercises

1. Animate a shape. Here's an opportunity to learn how to make shapes on a slide appear and disappear and get some practice on how appear/disappear animations work with groups. Here's a sample challenge:

    a.   Open your slideware application and create four shapes on a blank slide.

    b.   Make the first shape appear on mouse click.

    c.   Make the second and third ones appear together. (Hint: you can either use the grouping function to make shapes 2 and 3 into one object or program them to appear "with previous.")

    d.   Make the first three shapes disappear as the fourth appears.

2. Animate a list of text. You can add an animation to items in a list where you want the items to appear one at a time instead of all at once. This is a useful skill to add to your toolkit because at times you'll need to show a list of items but want students to focus on them one at a time. Find a slide from one of your existing decks that includes a nice long list, or create a slide that shows your grocery list. Now figure out how to add an "appear" animation to each item in the list.

All four of the slideware applications reviewed for this book have both a manual process for adding these animations and a shortcut method that uses one keystroke to add the same animation to multiple lines of text. Teach yourself both methods, and find a YouTube tutorial to help if you need it.

As another challenge, practice adding animations that disappear the previous item as the next one appears. This amount of animation programming is more difficult to achieve but can be worth it, especially for complex material.

Bullet Point Master Class

We've spent a great deal of time talking about reasons you might consider moving away from using bullet points as the main solution in your slide design toolkit. I want you to try other visual solutions first. However, bulleted text sometimes is the best choice. In this lesson, we'll talk about some scenarios in which bulleted slides are more efficient than other slide designs and how to do them right when you do use them. The main takeaway of this lesson should be that when you use bullet points, use them in a way that helps your students learn and remember.

Sometimes Bullets Are the Best Choice

Bullets sometimes are the best (read: most effective) design choice. Information on slides should be displayed as bullet points only sparingly, and only in situations where you are

- explaining one idea that has several supporting statements,

- showing an overview of a list of items that you plan to explicate individually in other slides, or

- providing a summary of items that you've already discussed.

Bulleted lists are sometimes helpful in showing a comprehensive list of representative examples where students don't need to memorize or retain the individual examples. Figure 14.1 accompanies a lecture on the economic importance of various members of the nightshade family. The point of the slide is not to have students memorize them, but rather to show the disparate genera in the potato family. (Figure 9.14 is another example.)

14.1

Students might understandably experience some degree of visual overwhelm when you present a slide like this to them. I'm not suggesting panic will ensue, but they might become momentarily distracted, either in wondering, *Ack! Am I supposed to copy all of this down?* or in homing in on the specific details, wondering, for example, to which of these genera the common dinner potato belongs. Because the effectiveness of visuals is part how they look and part how you interact with them, you'd likely mitigate overwhelm by managing expectations for what students are expected to do with the information on this slide.

Bullet Logic

Figure 14.2 depicts the logic error that typically occurs with improperly bulleted slides. One of the ideas presented beneath the main ideas really does support it, but the rest are either tangentially related or items the speaker hopes not to forget to mention.

All the information on this slide is technically related, but it isn't directly in service of the main idea, as the logical hierarchy of a heading and subpoints prescribes. In other words, the design is in conflict

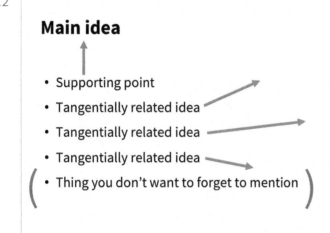

14.2

with the content. Therefore, although these items may all need to be mentioned verbally, not all of them need to appear on the slide. Again, things that appear on a slide are given value and importance by the fact that they are there at all, so you need to be both selective and intentional about what you include.

Bullets Done Right: Parallel Structure

Your bullet-pointed list should, instead, function logically as depicted in Figure 14.3.

14.3

Main idea

- Supporting point
- Supporting point
- Supporting point
- Supporting point

Here the arrangement of the content (supporting statements displayed beneath the main idea) results in a focused and concise slide with one well-supported main idea. This simple visual heuristic automatically eliminates bullet points as an option for those scenarios in which you might be lulled, tempted, or simply exhausted back into the ineffective practice of projecting lecture notes onto the screen.

Each bulleted supporting point should have the same relationship, grammatically and semantically, to the main idea. It's called *parallel structure*. When each bullet has the same relationship to the main idea, the student has fewer things to keep in working memory while taking in new information. Recall that it's not physically possible to read and listen at the same time, a condition that overloads working memory. Creating slides without logic errors mitigates that load. Let's look at a real-life slide to see what happens when students try to learn from a slide that has logic problems (Figure 14.4).

14.4

The lymphatic system

- Helps your body maintain homeostasis
- Is a network of vessels and organs that runs through your body
- Filters dead cells, viruses, bacteria and other unneeded particles from tissue fluid
- Absorbs tissue fluid that collects around cells
- Lymph vessels include lymph nodes
- The heart does not pump lymph through the body

From a semantic standpoint, the first four bullets each tell what the lymphatic system does. However, bullet five presents new information, switching the focus from what the lymphatic system does to naming physiological components of the system. This new focus forces the student to return to the main idea and establish a different understanding of it. Now the slide is talking not just about what the lymph system does, but about parts within the system as well. Bullet six provides yet more information; now this slide includes information about the functionality of the system. So the student has to return to the main idea again in order to figure out how to integrate the new information. Figure 14.5 uses arrows and brackets to depict where logic is parallel and where violations exist.

As you can see, when the main idea becomes unreliable for making quick sense of the supporting points, the student has to do more work, which nullifies any efficiencies that may have been gained from using bullets.

Finally, from a grammatical standpoint, only three of these six bullets (items one, three, and four) are parallel with the main idea. The nonparallel statements destroy the fluidity with which a student might read the slide.

In sum, bullets can be the most efficient way of presenting information but only when all the statements have the same relationship to the main idea.

14.5

The lymphatic system

- Helps your body maintain homeostasis
- Is a network of vessels and organs that runs through your body
- Filters dead cells, viruses, bacteria and other unneeded particles from tissue fluid
- Absorbs tissue fluid that collects around cells
- Lymph vessels include lymph nodes
- The heart does not pump lymph through the body

Bullet Economy

Bullets can be an efficient means of presenting information when they allow students to quickly apprehend the main idea. You can maximize this efficiency by ensuring that the main idea is appropriately descriptive in introducing the information that comes after it. The slide in Figure 14.6 is taken from a lecture about major figures of the Harlem Renaissance.

The repetition of reading "is credited with" three times not only taxes cognitive resources but also creates a distracting visual rhythm. These bullets each can be made more economical by moving the repetitive part of the statement to the title area of the slide, which creates a stronger introductory clause (Figure 14.7).

Now students can more efficiently apprehend the topic of this slide, freeing them to focus on the new information about Garvey's areas of influence.

14.6

Marcus Garvey

- is credited with spearheading the Back To Africa movement
- is credited with inspiring the Rastafari movement
- is credited with founding the Black Star Line

14.7

Marcus Garvey is credited with

- spearheading the Back To Africa movement

- inspiring the Rastafari movement

- founding the Black Star Line

Don't Make Bulleted or Numbered Lists Manually

The practical function of bullet points is to create white space, allowing the eye to distinguish more easily where each new idea begins.

You should always use the bullet point tool and let the slideware create the bullets for you rather than attempt to manually create a bullet effect using a symbol and your spacebar. What do I mean?

This list was created manually using the hyphen key and one space between the hyphen and the text:

- Point
- Point
- Point

These manually created bullets look crowded. And, it would be really easy for me to forget how many spaces I was using between bullet and text, which would make the list look less uniform.

By contrast, this list was created using the bullet autoformatting tool:

- Point
- Point
- Point

Notice the comfortable amount of space the software automatically inserted, both the indent from the page margin and between the bullet and text. From a workflow standpoint, autoformatted lists are easier to maintain, and they create more uniform, more appealing lists. Additionally, as discussed in Lesson 4, they make the list accessible for adaptive technology users.

For these reasons, you should let the software make your lists for you, which is better for everyone.

Protect the Space around Bullets

As discussed, one of the efficiencies of bullets is to assist in scanning. Bullets work well visually because of the positioning of shape (bullet) and white space, which allows the eye to move quickly from item to item within a list. Bullets are most effective when this white space is controlled. You want to pay attention to the white space wherever it occurs: between each bullet point, around the indented text, and between each item, especially where bullets contain more than one line of text.

Compare the inadequate and inconsistent bulleting in the left side of Figure 14.8 with the more uniform bulleting at right.

Adding consistent white space around each bullet and between each bulleted item, as well as indenting the text of each line, makes it much easier to scan this information, as you want students to be doing when they're listening to you.

14.8

Use the Right Type of List

The purposes of ordered (numbered) lists and bullet-pointed lists are different and, therefore, not interchangeable. Use ordered lists and bullet-pointed lists intentionally.

Ordered lists are most appropriate to show a process of steps that need to happen in a specific order. For example:

How to read a journal article:

1. Determine relevance: skim Abstract, Introduction, and Conclusion.
2. Read for understanding; carefully read all sections.
3. Scan References to inform additional literature searches.

An ordered list is also appropriate for lists that have a set number of items.

A sentence has two main parts:

1. Subject
2. Predicate

Last, an ordered list is an appropriate means of depicting items in order of importance or statistical hierarchy. For example:

Top five pregnancy-related causes of maternal deaths worldwide:

1. Hemorrhage (25%)
2. Infection (15%)
3. Unsafe abortion (13%)
4. Eclampsia (12%)
5. Obstructed labor (8%)

Bullet-pointed lists, by contrast, are best used to depict items that belong in the same category or that are subordinate, supportive points of a main idea.

Choose Appropriate, Standard Bullet Shapes

Bullets should serve to delineate your ideas, not draw attention to the bullets themselves. A clever use of bullets may serve a stylistic purpose. For example, a talk I once attended by pediatrician/magician Michael Pitt, MD, comes to mind; his talk on the use of magic tricks to help ease patient anxiety during medical exams included bullets in the shapes of diamonds, clubs, hearts, and spades, which successfully—and most importantly, subtly—evoked the magician motif. However, this choice also means you run the risk of distracting students. The way to tell if you've made an appropriate design decision is when the element in question disappears into the design, that is, when it looks integral and absolutely intentional. When any element sticks out, it's time to reassess its presence on the slide.

Likewise, don't rely on bullet point symbols to convey critical information, as was attempted in Figure 14.9, which lists the pros and cons of cow's milk consumption in humans.

14.9

PROs and CONs of cow's milk consumption in humans

★ Provides multiple key nutrients
★ Reduces risk of ischemic stroke/heart disease
★ Optimizes peak bone mass during adolescence
★ Speeds weight loss and reduces body fat

x Impairs ability to absorb iron
x Correlation between milk consumption and coronary heart disease
x One-third of adolescents are lactose intolerant
x No influence on weight loss or reduced body fat

The author used star-shaped bullets for the pros and X-shaped bullets for the cons. Using these symbols to convey the author's meaning is visually ineffective for several reasons. First, the star-as-pro and X-as-con conventions rely on a degree of familiarity with Western cultural symbols for things that are good and things that are bad. Choosing bullets that depend on a student's nuanced understanding of symbolic meaning leaves some students at an unfair disadvantage. Second, a screen reader won't read the difference between the star and X bullets, so the information embedded in them is lost for anyone who can't see or isn't looking at the slide. Third, because the visual distinctions between the stars and Xs are relatively minimal, even the most visually literate students might possibly miss altogether the distinctions between the pros and cons. A makeover (Figure 14.10) combines standard bullet shapes while making use of the left-right pro-con compositional expectation discussed in Lesson 10.

The standard small round dot or square at 75 percent of the size of the text is adequate for most bullet tasks. This is a decision best made once and captured in the Slide Master. As with any decision in academic slide design, choose the sparest, simplest, most efficient means of communication, and be consistent.

14.10

Cow's milk consumption by humans

PRO +	CON -
• Provides multiple key nutrients	• Impairs ability to absorb iron
• Reduces risk of ischemic stroke/heart disease	• May correlate with coronary heart disease
• Optimizes peak bone mass during adolescence	• One-third of adolescents are lactose intolerant
• Speeds weight loss and reduces body fat	• No influence on weight loss or reduced body fat

Bullets and Punctuation

In my circles, there is a healthy collegial debate about the use of punctuation in bullet-pointed lists on slides (and I do realize there are more important things going on in the world). Some say that a colon should follow every title heading just as it would in a print medium.

The projected slide isn't the same as the print medium, and rules of style don't always apply across both spaces. Some text-to-speech adaptive technologies do insert a longer pause when a colon or period is present than when there is none. However, the colon or period is also a stylistic choice. For instance, I argue that the size and visuo-spatial positioning of the title text, as well as the function of the title text placeholder, do the work of a colon in this design, making the colon redundant and therefore superfluous. However, the larger theme of this book is that your design decisions always be intentional and consistent. If you always use a colon, always use a colon, so it doesn't become a point of distraction for students who know your slides well.

Exercises

1. Learn how to control the indents and tabs in your slideware application. Your slideware offers you the ability to control both the indenting and space between items in a bulleted list. Find a YouTube tutorial that shows how to use the Ruler or Tabs controls to make these adjustments.

Make a bullet-pointed slide and practice adjusting the amount of space between margin and bullet and between bullet and text.

2. Examine your slide decks for bullet missteps.

In the way of reflecting on old habits and developing new skills, go back through some of your old slide decks, paying particular attention to the slides that contain a lot of bullet-pointed material. Answer these questions:

- How would you rate yourself at achieving a logical, parallel structure in most cases?

- Do you use ordered and unordered lists appropriately?

- Do you use standard bullet shapes (or can you articulate a strong stylistic reason to deviate from this recommendation)?

- How much, if any, information is encoded in the shape, size, or color of the bullets?

- Do you have adequate and consistent amounts of space in between the bullets, the indented text, and between each item that make the bulleted statements easy to differentiate?

Now, using these best practices as a guide, perform a makeover on one of your most egregiously bulleted slides, and marvel at the vastly improved slide you've just created.

Good Digital Citizenry

Good digital citizenry encompasses best practices for authors of digital content, like slide decks and handouts. As with any other academic writing, best practices include properly citing others' ideas, giving appropriate credit to the creators of the media we display in our designs, and including the date the material was created. Each of these practices has implications for what is included on the visible area of the slide canvas. This lesson gives suggestions for how you can show this information without interfering with the content of your designs. Additionally, I offer tips on how to make it easy for others to cite and reuse your slides. By the end of this short lesson, you'll have uncovered opportunities to share your new writing while responsibly reusing material created by others.

The First Slide

The first slide in your deck presents a number of opportunities to model good digital citizenry. Consider including these five elements on the first slide for every academic talk you give:

- A large, relevant, motivational graphic

- Title of the talk (obviously)

- Your name and contact information

- Date (either of the lecture or most recent content update)

- Your institutional logo (if applicable)

- A Creative Commons license (if desired)

Figure 15.1 shows an example of all these elements on a title slide. Let's talk about them in more detail.

15.1

Motivational Graphic

The principal pedagogical reason for including a graphic on the title slide is that a motivational image can help prime students and pique their interest in the topic. The image you choose should be either visually stunning or provide some other form of visual novelty. You want students to get excited about what you're about to present and to get a question in their heads: *How does this image relate to what I'm about to learn?* Don't waste this opportunity by selecting a generic image that doesn't say anything, such as that tired corporate stock photo imagery of people in suits. Be bold! Be creative!

Contact Information

It's a courtesy to students to provide not only the title of your talk but also your name and contact information on the first slide. I recommend that you add this information even if you address the same group of students three times a week; digital resources tend to persist in the environment, and you'll want students to be able to find and cite your work even years down the road, especially if you distribute your slide file rather than a handout.

Lecture Date or Date Last Updated

Similarly, providing the date that a particular lecture was delivered or last updated also serves as a courtesy to students. We use the date of publication of journal articles and academic textbooks to get a sense of general timeliness of information; likewise in a slide deck, providing that same information is helpful for diligent students who want to know when the information was written, reviewed, or updated. Here you have a valuable opportunity to communicate the fact that your content is vibrant, alive, and current. Make sure you update the date of the lecture for this semester's students, especially if you give the same talk semester after semester. This simple practice may help them organize their notes or retrieve the file when they're studying for the final. Finally, a lecture date is a relevant and important detail, should others choose to cite your lecture in their own work.

Logo

Your institutional logo belongs on the title slide and perhaps also on the end slide, and that's the only place it belongs. Recall from the discussion of illuminative versus decorative graphics in Lesson 8 that logos anywhere else in the deck are decoration and should be eliminated.

Creative Commons License (If Desired)

The Creative Commons initiative is a convenient way to let people know how you intend for your intellectual work to be used. You can specify any of several licenses. If you do elect to offer your work under a Creative Commons license, you can download an icon version of the license and display it on the title slide to call students' attention to it. For more information on licensing your work with a Creative Commons license, visit creativecommons.org.

End Matter Slides

End matter is a term borrowed from the print publishing industry, which refers to those pages at the end of a book that provide additional information about the work. End matter slides bookend the talk with information such as:

- Media credits

- Acknowledgments

- Recommended reading and resource lists

- Contact information that includes your online presence (website, Twitter handle, etc.)

Media Credits and Acknowledgments

To model best practices in share and share-alike of the film clips, images, and graphics used in your presentation, you should devote one or more slides at the end of your deck to credit the makers of that media. Beyond just a list, media credit slides can be made more recognizable and meaningful when a thumbnail of each is paired with the text of the credit (as in Figure 15.2). This isn't only a matter of treating others as you would want to be treated, it's also a clever record-keeping strategy for those times when you want to find and reuse an image but can't remember where you got it.

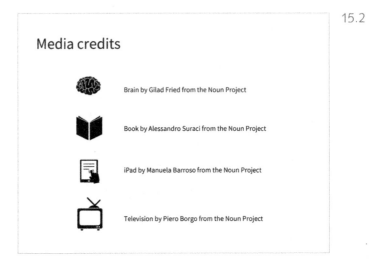

15.2

You can use the same visual treatment with acknowledgment slides as well. When you display pictures of the real people who provided assistance to you in your lecture preparation, you're showing gratitude as well as modeling collaboration and humanizing the collegial process: a three-fer!

Recommended Resources

An exhaustive list of references displayed in tiny print on one slide at the end of a long presentation is ineffective; students won't have time to read and copy them down, and you'll probably be annoyed having to copy and paste them from your word processing software and then reformatting them on the slides. The best format for providing a bibliography is via a handout that students can save and print (or not). Source citations also should be listed unobtrusively at the bottom of the slides they support. If you have a few carefully curated, key resources you'd really like students to look up, consider displaying them in a visual, memorable way, such as with pictures of book covers (Figure 15.3).

15.3

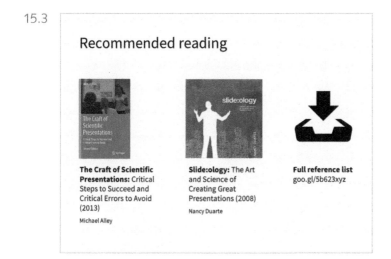

The Last Slide

The last slide in the deck provides a visual cue (for both speaker and students) that the prepared lecture section has ended. It usually also provides the backdrop for the question-and-answer session. For this reason, many lecturers intuitively use a one-word slide like "Questions?" or "Thank you!" to fulfill this purpose. But consider additional ways to leverage the extended view time this slide will receive. You may want to use it as an opportunity to cement one final point into their memory. You might redisplay an evocative image from your title slide, giving students the opportunity to reflect on the talk as a whole (Figure 15.4). Or you might simply use this slide to be a little bit clever,

15.4

helping relieve some of the tension built up over the course of an information-dense presentation (Figure 15.5).

In any case, the very last slide is a great place to include—again—your contact information and a link to your handout.

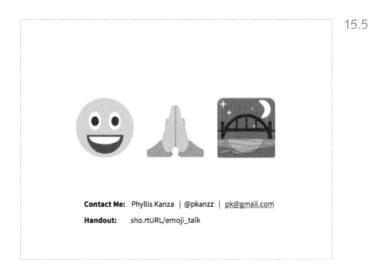

15.5

Cite Information Sources

As a matter of good digital citizenry and collegial academic practice, you should have a plan for how you will cite information sources. Pick a consistent location, color, and font size for this information, and stick with these decisions for the whole deck. As discussed, consistency helps students learn how to learn from your slides. As soon as they figure out that references are always at bottom left, slide numbers are always at bottom right, and media attributions are always on a slide near the end of the deck, they'll be able to easily distinguish these details from other content that also appears on the slide. They'll know where to look if they need that information, but it won't distract them from the rest of the instructional message.

Find Images for Instructional Use

As educators, we have the opportunity and the responsibility to set a strong example for students as digitally literate citizens of the information age. This responsibility includes modeling responsible image searches and use of digital resources, and methodically and consistently citing information sources. Although educators can claim fair use of images under some circumstances, that discussion is outside the scope of this book. Consider consulting your university's copyright and fair use resources for further guidance.

Royalty-Free Doesn't Mean Cost-Free

When doing an image search, the word *free* doesn't necessarily mean you don't have to pay someone in exchange for its use. Royalty-free images don't require you to pay a royalty fee to the image's creator. However, many times you do still have to pay a license fee to the company that distributes the image. What can you do instead?

Strategies for Finding Your Own Graphics

Fortunately, online search tools are becoming more sophisticated; both Bing and Google now allow you to narrow your image search results to just images that are licensed for use with attribution or use with modification. These search filters can help narrow your results, though you'll still need to find the original image source and make sure you know the terms of reuse. You can also try these strategies:

- **Utilize institutional media databases.** Your institution's library may maintain subscriptions to media databases. Because these databases often are subscription based, having an affiliation with a major research institution is a benefit, because it may be necessary to log in to gain access to the images. A librarian at your institution should be able to direct you to the subscription-based media databases available where you teach.

- **Utilize government databases.** Examples include the Centers for Disease Control and Prevention Public Health Image Library ("PHIL"). Paid for by federal tax dollars, we all have rights to use these images.

- **Perform a Creative Commons (CC) search.** When you search for images through this site, a Creative Commons Search (search.creativecommons.org) delimiter is automatically added to your query. As of this writing, the CC Search tool allows you to restrict your search results on a number of sites (e.g., YouTube, Flickr Commons, Wikipedia, Fotopedia, and others) to include only images that are free to use with attribution (or other specification). Again, though, make sure to consult the original image source to make sure you understand the terms of reuse.

- **Create your own images or graphics.** If creating, editing, cataloging, and storing your own graphics seems like a daunting amount of work without a lot of payoff, organize your colleagues to develop a shared library of images and graphics within your college or working unit.

- **Make your own line art.** Numerous mobile apps let you use your finger to draw on the device and export the drawing as an image file. If you prefer the old school approach, you can make line drawings in pen and scan them, then open them in a vector art program to convert them to digital vector art. Free web-based tools that perform this image-to-vector conversion are also available, such as vectormagic.com.

- **Search other free images databases.** There are a lot of good people in the world, and searching for free images on the web —actually free, with no use restrictions—will prove this to you. Two that I consult regularly are morguefile.com (for images) and openclipart.org (for vector art). Free sites like these are most useful for finding evocative images, so you may need to look elsewhere to find media suitable for instructional graphics.

Conference Hack:
They're Tweeting My Slides!

You've been invited to keynote a conference. You've spent months preparing your talk and taken pains to make sure your slides are impeccable. During the talk, you spend fourteen minutes building toward a brilliant, courageous, cleverly illustrated point.

Looking out at the blur of faces in the crowd, you realize that about half of them have their phones in the air taking a picture of your slide, a slide that took you months to come up with and that went through at least eight iterations during multiple rehearsals with coworkers and your spouse. You wish you'd written a hashtag for your talk because you know this moment is going to be epic on Twitter. But tragically you realize that this slide includes no visible credit to your intellectual labor; you were following the principles of academic slide design and you'd dutifully removed anything that could be considered superfluous. Now you're about to become Twitter-famous, but actually not really because there's no evidence of you on this slide. As your slide gets retweeted, it will eventually become detached from you.

Even though I'm still not an advocate for adding your institution's logo on the bottom of every single slide, I do think there comes a point when you know that one of your slides is pretty good. For those slides, consider unobtrusively including your name, institution, and Twitter handle, as depicted in Figure 15.6.

15.6

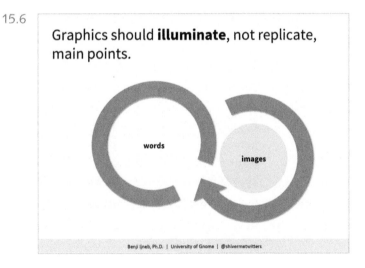

Social media aside, when someone from your audience decides they want to cite you in their blog post or dissertation in the future, finding you will be difficult. You can make it easier for them through thoughtfully placed self-attribution.

Sharing Your Content with the World

Presentation slides (and their accompanying handout) are perfect examples of intellectual work to include on a personal blog or teaching portfolio. Depending on your career and teaching goals, you might also find yourself utilizing a slide-sharing web service with a social media focus. The advantages of slide-sharing sites are the same as any social media site: ease of viewing, ability to embed in a learning management system, blog or portfolio website, and the ability for people to discover, like, comment, and share your work. Some slide-sharing sites let you indicate whether others may download your slides or a PDF of them.

For any of these sharing scenarios in which you choose to share your decks and handouts, you may want to consider adding metadata to the file. *Metadata* is a technical term for information that is stored invisibly within an electronic file. Computers read this information and use it to help you find files on your computer (among other things). You can access the metadata from the Properties panel of any electronic file, and you can even make changes to it. If you add information here, the metadata will travel with the file no matter where it gets downloaded. For instance, if you add your name and contact information in this space, your information will travel with it, even if it somehow gets deleted from the visible area of the document.

In addition to contact information, you might also consider adding learning objectives, a Creative Commons license (if you're using one), or additional context about the course or event for which you prepared the talk. In these ways, you can help ensure that others use your intellectual work as you intended, or at the very least, that the random person who stumbles across your work can connect with you if they want to. Use these strategies for both slides and handouts. The best approach is to send your files out into the world with as much embedded information in them as you can.

Exercises

1. Tags and keywords. Open the Properties panel of one of your slide decks and add a note with some nonsense word or phrase that you don't typically use (e.g., "unicorn soup"), and then save and close the file. Now go to your computer's search bar and search by the term that you added. Your file should appear in the results. This process is somewhat similar to the way in which search engines on the web look for keywords embedded in the metadata of web pages. This exercise also demonstrates a file organization strategy that can be useful on your local computer beyond the use of folders and file names.

2. Add metadata to a slide file. Open the Properties panel on your slide deck from within your slideware. Explore the fields in the panel and add whatever information you want, including your name, contact information, and keywords. After you add it, this metadata will be embedded in the deck and will travel along with it, even if the slide that lists your contact information gets deleted. Consider making this a habit if you electronically distribute either slide decks or handouts.

3. Explore Creative Commons licenses. Navigate to creativecommons.org and explore the different types of licenses. Think about which one you might want to use. Examine the human-readable verbiage that accompanies each license, as well as the embed code you can cut and paste into your portfolio website or blog. You also can download the icon that goes with each license, which you can add to your title slide.

4. Image search. Locate the image filter controls in your favorite search engine that let you narrow your search by specific parameters. Find an image that is labeled for reuse with attribution. Click through the search results to find the original source of the image, and verify whether that image really does have the type of license that you searched on. Consider ways you can contribute to a community of media and resource sharing. What new practices are you likely to adopt? How will you fit these practices into your workflows?

The Academic Slide Design Method

By now you've certainly realized that this book is not just about how to make better slides, but also about how making better slides results in better lectures. For one thing, you'll interact with your slides differently during your lecture, no longer reading from them word for word like a teleprompter. Students will interact with your lectures differently, too. They'll no longer sit passively with a copy of the slide deck during your lectures, because by necessity they'll need to be taking more notes. As a result, they'll be more actively, physically engaged with what you're saying. Additionally, they'll no longer skip class, because they won't assume they can get the whole lecture by reading a copy of the slides. The slides no longer are the lecture. A new way of writing, organizing, and delivering lectures calls for a new method of designing slides, and in this last lesson we'll talk about that process.

The Method, in Brief

For academic slide design, you can no longer just open up your slideware application and start cranking out slides. You'll need to turn your typical lecture-planning process on its head. Here's the academic slide design method in a nutshell:

1. Write a script.

2. Prepare the handout.

3. Identify and sketch the visuals.

4. Create the slides in the slideware.

5. Add preview and guidepost slides.

6. Test and iterate.

Notice how the manual labor of actually creating the slides comes further along in the slide design process—perhaps, for some, disconcertingly further along. Especially if that conference you're presenting at is next week, the sensation of "wasting time" writing a script, creating a handout, and storyboarding may cause some angst. Having prepared presentations both ways, I can attest to the fact that planning first and making the slides later results not only in a stronger presentation but also in less time spent futzing with the slides. I promise.

Write a Script

Seriously consider scripting your talk start to finish, word for word. I hear some of you laughing, but believe me when I say that this step is exactly the opposite of a waste of time.

To a busy instructor, the idea of scripting a talk may seem preposterous—especially if you're a seasoned, tenured faculty member who has been giving the same lecture for years. You know what you're going to say already; you don't need to write it down! Reading from a script sounds clunky and unnatural! You don't have time to write your script; in the time it will take you to write it, you could have spoken it twice over.

I've heard all these arguments before, and I offer eight counterarguments:

1. Writing is thinking, an act of discovery and of organizing ideas, best suited to a word processing document or pen and paper rather than a slide. Back in the days before reading this book, when you used to try and combine writing (thinking) with the visual task of slide design, you probably discovered more than once that the last bullet point on your slide was, in fact, the essential point you wanted to make.

The preceding bullet points were the stuff you needed to process before you arrived at and identified the main point.

2. Writing is a holistic activity, whereas presentation software by definition breaks ideas up into chunks. Your lecture will flow better if you can see it all in one place as you're creating it rather than broken up across a bunch of slides (where it's also tempting to start tweaking and rearranging things, which is a waste of time at this stage).

3. Writing a script for a talk you've given in the past can help you see your old content with new eyes, perhaps highlighting opportunities to refresh it.

4. Writing a script for a brand-new talk can help you make sure that your goals, themes, and language are appropriate to the level and expertise of your next audience. You'll find places you need to build out more examples or more evidence. You'll identify points that need to be added. You'll discover superfluous threads that can be omitted because they don't actually support the main idea.

5. Rehearsing from a script can reduce your reliance on slides as a teleprompter, which reduces your dependence on bullet points as a design idea, freeing up the real estate on your slides for more cognitively efficient practices, such as illuminative visual evidence. I'm not recommending you read a script aloud to your students but just that you work from it while designing the slides.

6. Scripting creates an instant transcript, which you can provide as a separate learning resource that will be appreciated by students of all abilities and levels, especially those who are working in their second language. You can also use the transcript to create closed captions if your lecture is being recorded for the web.

7. Speaking of recorded lectures, as more and more are produced, a script makes audio editing so much easier. In a live audience situation, people are usually able to overlook the speaker's fillers (umm, ah, so, etc.), but in a recording

the filler words are amplified and should be edited out. Besides it being a time-consuming process, too much of this type of editing can, on the whole, degrade the quality of the recording. If you're reading from a script, your recording will include fewer verbal missteps.

8. If an instructional designer is working with you to help create the visuals, a script will help them be able to work more effectively on your behalf. It's impossible to do the structural work of slide design or even a good makeover without benefit of the full picture of what will be covered in the talk, and you'd be surprised how often the key idea that the speaker wants to communicate actually isn't visually represented in the bulleted slides.

Beyond these, writing a script can help give you the personal assurance that you'll have covered everything you'd set out to, organized and articulated just as you'd intended.

Prepare the Handout

In addition to advocating that you write a script of your talk, I also want to encourage you to create a separate, concise document to distribute as a handout.

As with the script, taking the time and care to identify all the main ideas first before moving into the slideware will save you exponential amounts of time later in the visual design process. Creating a separate handout can help free you from the impulse to place all of your content onto the slide canvas (thus also saving students from having to view a bunch of text-heavy slides), but it has additional benefits as well, as outlined in Lesson 4.

Identify and Sketch the Visuals

Identify places in the script where the content would be illuminated by a combination of verbal information and some type of visual. As discussed throughout this book, the purpose of a visual aid is to illuminate—not decorate, not replicate, not merely evoke the idea of—the concepts of your lecture. After you've identified those areas you believe would benefit from visual aids, you'll want to do some storyboarding, which is just a fancy way of saying, grab a pen and paper and sketch them out.

Why pen and paper? Slideware is by definition a "finishing medium," designed to help you produce the final product. It wasn't designed to help you mock up a bunch of possible design ideas. So, if you've ever resented your slideware for being difficult to use and ultimately a big hassle, perhaps it's because you weren't using it for its intended purpose.

Visual designs are iterative in the same way that drafts of written work are iterative: your first attempt at an illuminative design may fail, and multiple versions may be required in order to arrive at the final, most effective solution. Pen and paper will always save you time in the long run, and I'd venture to argue (though I have no way to prove it) that that more tactile, less bounded medium also will free you to come up with better designs.

Once you get familiar with the process of thinking visually, you'll eventually be able to fast-forward some of this storyboarding process. When I'm writing my scripts, I'm often also making notes to myself as I type, **[which I place in boldface and brackets to remind myself of places I'd like to add a visual]**. The storyboarding process could be as easy as that, depending on your subject matter.

Even still, I do all of this thinking and planning before I open my slideware application. It bears reiteration: the creation of effective visual aids will *always* end up taking less time if you suppress the impulse to just start cranking out the slides.

Create the Slides in the Slideware

The heavy lifting is behind you. You've identified the main themes and ideas of your talk and planned the slides you want to create. Now all that's left is a few clicks in the slideware to make your visual designs a reality. This step is also where you'll use the animation tool to create progressive disclosures and annotations (see Lesson 13).

Add Preview and Guidepost Slides

Students in live lecture situations will benefit from seeing a couple of visuals that show them what they're about to learn, as well as being reminded throughout the talk about where they are. This practice supports attention and retention of key information and is true for students of all levels, from undergraduates to professionals. When you're first getting used to the academic slide design method, it likely will be easiest and most efficient to add preview and guidepost slides after you've built the rest of the deck. That way you'll be able to see the big picture of your presentation and think about pacing.

Test and Iterate

A slide design that's perfectly obvious to you may be completely mis-interpreted by students. That's why testing them with a colleague or, preferably, with a student is a good idea. Doing so is the surest way to evaluate whether the slide and the deck communicate what you intend. Testing will help prevent you from showing ineffective or—worse—confusing designs. It's also a great opportunity to practice how you deliver the talk *using* the slides.

I want to share with you a slide makeover I attempted and botched. I had listened to a recording of this lecture and studied the instructor's original slide (Figure 16.1). My makeover is shown in Figure 16.2.

I designed the makeover slide and returned to it a week later. I didn't need to talk it through with any colleagues; I knew that my design was off, because I could no longer articulate my original reasons for anything I'd done. Why the cog shape? Why its prominence as the most salient part of the design? Most importantly, what did the visual evidence have to do—at all—with the assertion? My failed makeover follows many of the best practices of academic slide design, but the visual solution was completely obscure.

I'll confess that I didn't sketch this design first; I made it right in the slideware, and that shortcut may also have contributed to the lack of success of the final product. Perhaps this subject didn't need a slide at all, and that's why it was difficult.

Design is always, always iterative.

Letting Go

It's easy to get protective of a design that you're especially proud of or that took you a long time to make. Some of those designs will be dif-ficult to get rid of for that reason; they've become your little darlings. I like to keep my little darlings in the slide deck alongside their more successful daughters and cousins. I simply hide them so they don't show up in presentation mode. Eventually I find I don't need them anymore, and I can delete them. As in life, a little emotional distance can go a long way toward letting go of something that just isn't working out.

16.1

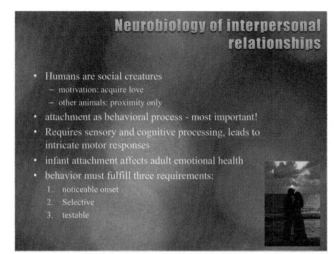

16.2

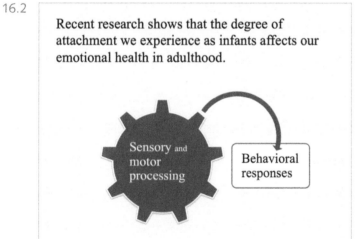

Exercises

1. Create and store your handout in the cloud. Create a handout to accompany one of your upcoming lectures and find a place in the cloud to put it. Some places you might store your handout include your website or blog, a file-sharing service (such as Dropbox or Google Drive), or your institution's learning management system. Figure out how to copy the URL of the handout so you can send the link to your students. For a bonus point, use a URL shortening service to shorten the length of the hyperlink and distribute that link to students instead.

2. Design a new lecture that follows this method. Next time you embark on the thrilling journey that is writing a new lecture, give the academic slide design method a try! Along the way, check in with yourself and see how this process feels compared to your old method of lecture planning and preparation. Which method felt more efficient? Which method resulted in the best deck? Which method resulted in the best lecture? How can you incorporate the academic slide design method into your future workflows?

Principles of Academic Slide Design

As a review of the ideas introduced throughout these sixteen lessons, I want to send you off with a list of seven easily digestible principles and twenty-two recommendations for academic slide design. If you like, this list could function as a checklist for your future slide design work. Armed as you are now, with a greater understanding of why some visual design practices are effective and some are not, you're free to follow, develop, or disregard them as your personal constitution and context dictate.

Principle 1: Support the functional needs of students.

1. Provide a handout that summarizes important information, formatted for accessibility (or an appropriately prepared version of the slide deck, alternatively).

2. Create strong contrasts of color, shape, type, and size.

3. Show the entirety of a complex structure prior to zooming in on any given part.

4. Use preview, guidepost, and recap slides to help students
    know where they are within the context of the lecture and
    to reinforce key messages.

Principle 2: Employ a consistent, simple, predictable, visual system that students must learn only once.

5. Choose four colors and stick with them for your entire deck.

6. Choose one typeface and stick with it for your entire deck.

7. Use a consistent style of graphics.

8. Select consistent locations for recurring pieces of content
    (citations, media credits, and slide numbers).

Principle 3: Provide illuminative visuals rather than decorative or redundant visuals.

9. Identify one main point per slide.

10. Select graphics that illuminate, enhance, or augment
    rather than replicate or simply evoke your main point.

Principle 4: Arrange elements on the slide canvas for efficient visual perception.

11. Create and preserve ample white space in your designs.

12. Visually distinguish key information from subordinate
    or supporting information.

13. Clearly show which information belongs together, is connected, and is separate.

14. Use predefined layouts to add content to slides.

15. For complex graphics, place labels as close as possible to the structures they label.

Principle 5: Reduce each visual solution to its essential information-carrying elements.

16. Strip the theme and start with a blank canvas.

17. Remove decoration in all its forms.

Principle 6: Use animations and annotations to guide attention.

18. Use animations to conceal content until you're ready to talk about it.

19. Use signaling techniques to help students focus on complex content.

Principle 7: Be a good digital citizen.

20. Include your contact information in your slides and handouts as well as in the metadata of these files.

21. Cite all media and include references to source information.

22. Consider using a Creative Commons license to help people know how to use your work.

Further Reading

As noted at the start, a number of comprehensive, worthwhile resources on slide design already exist. These four books approach the problem from different angles, and I recommend each for different reasons. None of them is specific to the context of classroom teaching, but each makes an important contribution toward the goal of teaching visual literacies.

Robin Williams's classic *The Non-Designer's Design Book* is useful background for anyone who does visual communication for a living. A natural teacher, Williams frames the problems and issues all designers face in their day-to-day communication in an entertaining, easy-to-read manner, accompanied by carefully selected examples that show as well as tell.

Michael Alley's *The Craft of Scientific Presentations: Critical Steps to Succeed and Critical Errors to Avoid* is a practical guide that helps the expert appropriately refine the lecture so that the listener can follow along. He's also one of the original evangelizers of the assertion-evidence technique, making him a celebrity in my mind.

For more advanced ideas on the topic of graphic design for the slide canvas, check out *Slide:ology: The Art and Science of Creating Great Presentations* by Nancy Duarte. This beautiful book provides inspiration and practical design guides for the advanced PowerPoint user (or the PowerPoint user with a talented assistant or design team). You'll want to own a copy that you can reference for years to come.

Connie Malamed's *Visual Design Solutions: Principles and Creative Inspiration for Learning Professionals* will take your visual literacy skills to the next level. Richly illustrated and written for the layperson, this book will help you grow your design skills in all types of teaching and learning contexts.

Works Consulted

All URLs were active at the time this book was published.

Abela, Andrew. *Advanced Presentations by Design: Creating Communication That Drives Action*. San Francisco: John Wiley & Sons, 2008.

Adams, Catherine. "On the 'Informed Use' of PowerPoint: Rejoining Vallance and Towndrow." *Journal of Curriculum Studies* 39, no. 2 (2007): 229–33.

———. "PowerPoint, Habits of Mind, and Classroom Culture." *Journal of Curriculum Studies* 38, no. 4 (2006): 389–411.

———. "PowerPoint's Pedagogy." *Phenomenology & Practice* 2, no. 1 (2008): 63–79.

———. "Teachers Building Dwelling Thinking with Slideware." *Indo-Pacific Journal of Phenomenology* 1, no. 10 (2010): 1–12.

Alley, Michael. *The Craft of Scientific Presentations*, 2nd ed. New York: Springer, 2013.

———, and Kathryn Neeley. "Rethinking the Design of Presentation Slides: A Case for Sentence Headlines and Visual Evidence." *Technical Communication* 4, no. 52 (2005): 417–26.

———, et al. "How the Design of Headlines in Presentation Slides Affects Audience Retention." *Technical Communication* 53, no. 2 (2006): 225–34.

Anderson, Terry, and Jon Dron. "Three Generations of Distance Education Pedagogy." *International Review of Research in Open and Distance Learning* 12, no. 3 (2011): 80–97.

Austin, Katharine. "Multimedia Learning: Cognitive Individual Differences and Display Design Techniques Predict Transfer Learning with Multimedia Learning Modules." *Computers & Education* 53, no. 4 (2009): 1,339–54.

Azer, Samy. "What Makes A Great Lecture? Use of Lectures in a Hybrid PBL Curriculum." *The Kaohsiung Journal of Medical Sciences* 25, no. 3 (2009): 109–15.

Barry, Ann Marie. "Perception Theory." In Kenneth L. Smith et al., eds. *Handbook of Visual Communication: Theory, Methods and Media, Handbook of Visual Communication: Theory, Methods, and Media.* New York: Routledge, 2004.

Bartsch, Robert, and Kristi Cobern. "Effectiveness of PowerPoint Presentations in Lectures." *Computers & Education* 41, no. 1 (2003): 77–86.

Bean, Joshua. "Presentation Software Supporting Visual Design: Displaying Spatial Relationships with a Zooming User Interface." In *Professional Communication Conference, IPCC 2012*, pp. 1–6. IEEE International.

Bergen, Lori, et al. "How Attention Partitions Itself during Simultaneous Message Presentations." *Human Communication Research* 31 no. 3 (2005): 311–36.

Berk, Ronald. "Research on PowerPoint: From Basic Features to Multimedia." *International Journal of Technology in Teaching and Learning* 7, no. 1 (2011): 24–35.

Birdsell, David, and Leo Groarke. "Outlines of a Theory of Visual Argument." *Argumentation and Advocacy* 43, no. 3/4 (2007): 103–13.

Block, Bruce A. *The Visual Story: Creating the Visual Structure of Film, TV, and Digital Media.* 2nd ed. Burlington, MA.: Focal Press, 2008.

Blokzijl, Wim. "The Effect of Text Slides Compared to Visualizations on Learning and Appreciation in Lectures." In *Professional Communication Conference, IPCC 2007*, pp. 1–9. IEEE International.

Bozarth, Jane. *Better Than Bullet Points: Creating Engaging e-Learning with PowerPoint.* Hoboken, NJ: John Wiley & Sons, 2013.

Bradshaw, Amy C. "Effects of Presentation Interference in Learning with Visuals." *Journal of Visual Literacy* 23, no. 1 (2003): 41–68.

Bransford, John D., Ann L. Brown, and Rodney R. Cocking, eds. *How People Learn: Brain, Mind, Experience, and School.* Washington, DC: National Academy Press, 2000.

Buttigieg, Pier. "Perspectives on Presentation and Pedagogy in Aid of Bioinformatics Education." *Briefings in Bioinformatics* 11, no. 6 (2010): 587–97.

Carney, Russell, and Joel Levin. "Pictorial Illustrations Still Improve
    Students' Learning from Text." *Educational Psychology Review* 14, no. 1
    (2002): 5–26.

Casteleyn, Jordi, André Mottart, and Martin Valcke. "The Impact of
    Graphic Organisers on Learning from Presentations." *Technology,
    Pedagogy and Education* 22, no. 3 (2013): 283–301.

Chapman, Jocelyn. "The Pragmatics and Aesthetics of Knowing:
    Implications for Online Education." *Kybernetes* 42, no. 8 (2013):
    1,166–80.

Clark, Ruth, and Chopeta Lyons. *Graphics for Learning: Proven Guidelines
    for Planning, Designing, and Evaluating Visuals in Training Materials.*
    Hoboken, NJ: John Wiley & Sons, 2010.

———, and Gary Harrelson. "Designing Instruction That Supports
    Cognitive Learning Processes." *Journal of Athletic Training* 37, no. 4
    suppl. (2002): S–152.

———, and Richard Mayer. *E-Learning and the Science of Instruction: Proven
    Guidelines for Consumers and Designers of Multimedia Learning.*
    Hoboken, NJ: John Wiley & Sons, 2016.

———. "Using Rich Media Wisely." In *Trends and Issues in Instructional
    Design and Technology*, pp. 309–20. Robert A. Reiser and John V.
    Dempsey, eds. 3rd. ed. Boston: Pearson, 2012.

Cook, David, et al. "Instructional Design Variations in Internet-Based
    Learning for Health Professions Education: A Systematic Review and
    Meta-Analysis." *Academic Medicine* 85, no. 5 (2010): 909–22.

Cooke, Lynne. "Eye Tracking: How It Works and How It Relates to
    Usability." *Technical Communication* 52, no. 4 (2005): 456–63.

Dake, Dennis M. "A Natural Visual Mind: The Art and Science of Visual
    Literacy." *Journal of Visual Literacy* 27, no. 1 (2007): 7–28.

Dirksen, Julie. *Design for How People Learn.* San Francisco: New Riders,
    2015.

Djonov, Emilia, and Theo van Leeuwen. "Between the Grid and
    Composition: Layout in PowerPoint's Design and Use." *Semiotica* 197
    (2013): 1–34.

Dondis, Donis A. *A Primer of Visual Literacy.* Cambridge, MA: MIT Press,
    1974.

Doumont, Jean-Luc. "The Cognitive Style of PowerPoint: Slides Are Not All
    Evil." *Technical Communication* 52, no. 1 (2005): 64–70.

———. "Creating Effective Presentation Slides." *OPN Optics & Photonics
    News* (March 2011): 12–14.

———. "Creating Effective Slides: Design, Construction, and Use in
    Science." Stanford University, April 19, 2013. http://www.youtube.com
    /watch?v=meBXuTIPJQk.

Duarte, Nancy. *Slide:ology: The Art and Science of Creating Great Presentations.* Toronto: O'Reilly Media, 2008.

Fleming, Malcolm, and Howard Levie. *Instructional Message Design: Principles from the Behavioral Sciences.* 2nd ed. Englewood Cliffs, NJ: Educational Technology Publications, 1993.

Gagne, Robert. "Mastery Learning and Instructional Design." *Performance Improvement Quarterly* 1, no. 1 (1988): 7–18.

Garner, Joanna, and Michael Alley. "How the Design of Presentation Slides Affects Audience Comprehension: A Case for the Assertion-Evidence Approach." *International Journal of Engineering Education* 29, no. 6 (2013): 1,564–79.

———. "PowerPoint in the Psychology Classroom: Lessons from Multimedia Learning Research." *Psychology Learning & Teaching* 10, no. 2 (2011): 95–106.

———. "Slide Structure Can Influence the Presenter's Understanding of the Presentation's Content." *International Journal of Engineering Education* 32, no. 1A (2016): 39–54.

Garner, Joanna, et al. "Assertion-Evidence Slides Appear to Lead to Better Comprehension and Recall of More Complex Concepts." Paper presented at the American Society for Engineering Education Annual Conference and Exposition 2011. https://www.asee.org/public /conferences/1/papers/900/view.

———. "A Cognitive Psychology Perspective." *Technical Communication* 56, no. 4 (2009): 331–45.

Gendelman, Joel. *Virtual Presentations That Work.* New York: McGraw-Hill, 2010.

Gier, Vicki, and David Kreiner. "Incorporating Active Learning with PowerPoint-Based Lectures Using Content-Based Questions." *Teaching of Psychology* 36, no. 2 (2009): 134–39.

Griffin, Darren, et al. "Podcasting by Synchronising PowerPoint and Voice: What Are the Pedagogical Benefits?" *Computers & Education* 53, no. 2 (2009): 532–39.

Gross, Alan, and Joseph Harmon. The Structure of PowerPoint Presentations: The Art of Grasping Things Whole. *Professional Communication, IEEE Transactions* 52, no. 2 (2009): 121–37.

Grunwald, Tiffany, and Charisse Corsbie-Massay. "Guidelines for Cognitively Efficient Multimedia Learning Tools: Educational Strategies, Cognitive Load, and Interface Design." *Academic Medicine* 81, no. 3 (2006): 213–23.

Guo, Philip, et al. "How Video Production Affects Student Engagement: An Empirical Study of MOOC Videos." In *Proceedings of the First ACM Conference on Learning @ Scale Conference,* March 4–5, 2014, pp. 41–50.

Hegarty, Mary. "The Cognitive Science of Visual-Spatial Displays: Implications for Design." *Topics in Cognitive Science* 3, no. 3 (2011): 446–74.

Hillman, Daniel, et al. "Learner-Interface Interaction in Distance Education: An Extension of Contemporary Models and Strategies for Practitioners." *American Journal of Distance Education* 8, no. 2 (1994): 30–42.

Horn, Robert. *Visual Language.* Bainbridge Island, WA: MacroVU, Inc., 1998.

Horvath, Jared. "The Neuroscience of PowerPoint." *Mind, Brain and Education* 8, no. 3 (2014): 137–43.

Issa, Nabil, et al. "Applying Multimedia Design Principles Enhances Learning in Medical Education." *Medical Education* 45, no. 8 (2011): 818–26.

Jamet, Eric. "An Eye-Tracking Study of Cueing Effects in Multimedia Learning." *Computers in Human Behavior* 32 (2014): 47–53.

———, and Olivier Le Bohec. "The Effect of Redundant Text in Multimedia Instruction." *Contemporary Educational Psychology* 32, no. 4 (2007): 588–98.

———, et al. "Attention Guiding in Multimedia Learning." *Learning and Instruction* 18, no. 2 (2008): 135–45.

Johnson, Douglas, and Jack Christensen. "A Comparison of Simplified–Visually Rich and Traditional Presentation Styles." *Teaching of Psychology* 38, no. 4 (2011): 293–97.

Johnson, Fred. "Film School for Slideware: Film, Comics, and Slideshows as Sequential Art." *Computers and Composition* 29, no. 2 (2012): 124–36.

Kahn, Paul, and Krzysztof Lenk. "Design: Principles of Typography for User Interface Design." *Interactions* 5, no. 6 (1998): 15.

———. "Screen Typography: Applying Lessons of Print to Computer Displays." *Seybold Report on Desktop Publishing* 7, no. 11 (1993): 3–15.

Kalyuga, Slava, et al. "When Redundant On-Screen Text in Multimedia Technical Instruction Can Interfere with Learning." *Journal of the Human Factors and Ergonomics Society* 46, no. 3 (2005): 567–81.

Kirschner, Femke, Liesbeth Kester, and Gemma Corbalan. "Cognitive Load Theory and Multimedia Learning, Task Characteristics, and Learning Engagement: The Current State of the Art." *Computers in Human Behavior* 27, no. 1 (2010): 1–4.

Kirschner, Paul, et al. "Contemporary Cognitive Load Theory Research: The Good, the Bad and the Ugly." *Computers in Human Behavior* 27, no. 1 (2011): 99–105.

Kissane, Erin. *The Elements of Content Strategy.* New York, NY: A Book Apart, 2011.

Kosslyn, Stephen M. *Better PowerPoint: Quick Fixes Based on How Your Audience Thinks.* New York: Oxford University Press, 2012.

———. *Clear and to the Point: 8 Psychological Principles for Compelling PowerPoint Presentations.* New York: Oxford University Press, 2007.

———, et al. "PowerPoint Presentation Flaws and Failures: A Psychological Analysis." *Frontiers in Psychology* 3 (2012): 1–22.

Kress, Gunther, and Theo van Leeuwen. *Reading Images: The Grammar of Visual Design.* 2nd ed. New York: Routledge, 2006.

Larkin, Jill, and Herbert Simon. "Why a Diagram Is (Sometimes) Worth Ten Thousand Words." *Cognitive Science* 11, no. 1 (1987): 65–100.

Lee, Chien-Ching. "Specific Guidelines for Creating Effective Visual Arguments in Technical Handouts." *Technical Communication* 58, no. 2 (2011): 135–48.

Levasseur, David, and J. Kanan Sawyer. "Pedagogy Meets PowerPoint: A Research Review of the Effects of Computer-Generated Slides in the Classroom." *Review of Communication* 6, no. 1–2: (2006): 101–23.

Levin, Joel R. "On Functions of Pictures in Prose." In Francis J. Pirozzolo and Merlin C. Wittrock, eds. *Neuropsychological and Cognitive Processes in Reading.* Cambridge, MA: Academic Press, 1981.

Levinson, Anthony. "Where Is Evidence-Based Instructional Design in Medical Education Curriculum Development?" *Medical Education* 44, no. 6 (2010): 536–37.

Lidwell, William, et al. *Universal Principles of Design: 125 Ways to Enhance Usability, Influence Perception, Increase Appeal, Make Better Design Decisions, and Teach through Design.* Beverly, MA: Rockport Publishers, 2010.

Lohr, Linda. *Creating Graphics for Learning and Performance: Lessons in Visual Literacy.* Upper Saddle River, NJ: Prentice Hall, 2007.

Mackiewicz, Jo. "Audience Perceptions of Fonts in Projected PowerPoint Text Slides." In *Professional Communication Conference, IPCC 2006*, pp. 68–76. IEEE International.

Manning, Alan, and Nicole Amare. "Visual-Rhetoric Ethics: Beyond Accuracy and Injury." *Technical Communication* 53, no. 2 (2006): 195–211.

Mayer, Richard E. "Elements of a Science of e-Learning." *Journal of Educational Computing Research* 29, no. 3 (2003): 297–13.

———. "Learning Strategies for Making Sense out of Expository Text: The SOI Model for Guiding Three Cognitive Processes in Knowledge Construction." *Educational Psychology Review* 8, no. 4 (1996): 357–71.

———. "Research-Based Principles for Designing Multimedia Instruction."
In Victor A. Benassi, Catherine E. Overson, and Christopher M. Hakala. *Applying Science of Learning in Education: Infusing Psychological Science into the Curriculum.* 2014. http://teachpsych.org/ebooks /asle2014/index.php.

———. "Research-Based Principles for Multimedia Learning." Harvard Initiative for Learning and Teaching, May 5, 2014. https://youtu.be /AJ3wSf-ccXo.

———, ed. *Cambridge Handbook of Multimedia Learning.* 2nd ed. New York: Cambridge University Press, 2014.

Mayer, Richard, and Roxana Moreno. "Nine Ways to Reduce Cognitive Load in Multimedia Learning." *Educational Psychologist* 38, no. 1 (2003): 43–52.

McKeachie, Wilbert, and Marilla Svinicki. "How to Make Lectures More Effective." In *McKeachie's Teaching Tips*, pp. 58–72. Boston: Cengage Learning, 2013.

Middendorf, Joan, and Alan Kalish. "The 'Change-Up' in Lectures." *National Teaching and Learning Forum* 5, no. 2 (1996): 1–5.

Munzner, Tamara. "Information Visualization Basics: 15 Views of a Node-Link Graph: An Information Visualization Presentation". Google Tech Talks, June 28, 2006. https://youtu.be/lDltGVQp8bE.

Nash, Susan Smith. "Learning Objects." In R. A. Reiser and J. V. Dempsey, eds. *Trends and Issues in Instructional Design and Technology.* New York: Pearson, 2011.

Neeley, Kathryn, et al. "Challenging the Common Practice of PowerPoint at an Institution." *Technical Communication* 56, no. 4 (2009): 346–60.

Nielsen, Jakob. "Banner Blindness: Old and New Findings." Nielsen Norman Group, August 20, 2007. https://www.nngroup.com/articles /banner-blindness-old-and-new-findings/.

Norman, Donald A. "Emotion and Design: Attractive Things Work Better." *Interactions Magazine* 9, no. 4 (2002): 36–42.

Paivio, Alan, et al. "Why Are Pictures Easier to Recall Than Words?" *Psychonomic Science* 11, no. 4 (1968): 137–38.

Parrish, Patrick. "Aesthetic Principles for Instructional Design." *Educational Technology Research and Development* 57, no. 4 (2009): 511–28.

———. "Design as Storytelling." *TechTrends* 50, no. 4 (2006): 72–82.

Peters, Dorian. *Interface Design for Learning: Design Strategies for Learning Experiences.* San Francisco: New Riders, 2014.

Pettersson, Rune. "Information Design—Principles and Guidelines." *Journal of Visual Literacy* 29, no. 2 (2010): 167–82.

———. "Visual Literacy and Message Design." *TechTrends* 53, no. 2 (2009): 3,840.

Reynolds, Garr. *Presentation Zen: Simple Ideas on Presentation Design and Delivery.* San Francisco: New Riders, 2011.

Ritzhaupt, Albert, et al. "The Effects of Time-Compressed Audio and Verbal Redundancy on Learner Performance and Satisfaction." *Computers and Human Behavior* 24 (2008): 2,434–45.

Ruiz, Jorge, et al. "The Impact of e-Learning in Medical Education." *Academic Medicine* 81, no. 3 (2006): 207–12.

Sadoski, Mark, and Allan Paivio. *Imagery and Text: A Dual Coding Theory of Reading and Writing.* New York: Routledge, 2013.

Santas, Ari, and Lisa Eaker. "The Eyes Know It? Training the Eyes: A Theory of Visual Literacy." *Journal of Visual Literacy* 28, no. 2 (2009): 163–85.

Savoy, April, Robert W. Proctor, and Gavriel Salvendy, "Information Retention from PowerPoint and Traditional Lectures." *Computers & Education* 52, no. 4 (2009): 858–67.

Schnotz, Wolfgang, and Christian Kürschner. "A Reconsideration of Cognitive Load Theory." *Educational Psychology Review* 19, no. 4 (2007): 469–508.

Slykhuis, David, et al. "Eye-Tracking Students' Attention to PowerPoint Photographs in a Science Education Setting." *Journal of Science Education and Technology* 14, no. 5–6 (2005): 509–20.

Son, Jinok, et al. "Effects of Visual-Verbal Redundancy and Recaps on Television News Learning." *Journal of Broadcasting & Electronic Media* 31, no. 2 (1987): 207–16.

Stephenson, Julia, et al. "Electronic Delivery of Lectures in the University Environment: An Empirical Comparison of Three Delivery Styles." *Computers & Education* 50, no. 3 (2008): 640–51.

Sugar, William, Abbie Brown, and Kenneth Luterbach. "Examining the Anatomy of a Screencast: Uncovering Common Elements and Instructional Strategies." *International Review of Research in Open and Distance Learning* 11, no. 3 (2010): 1–20.

Swarts, Jason. "New Modes of Help: Best Practices for Instructional Video." *Technical Communication* 59, no. 3 (2012): 195–206.

Sweller, John, et al. "Cognitive Architecture and Instructional Design." *Educational Psychology Review* 10, no. 3 (1998): 251–96.

Tangen, Jason, et al. "The Role of Interest and Images in Slideware Presentations." *Computers & Education* 56, no. 3 (2011): 865–72.

Tractinsky, Noam. "Toward the Study of Aesthetics in Information Technology." *ICIS 2004 Proceedings*, pp. 771–80.

Tufte, Edward R. *Beautiful Evidence.* Cheshire, CT: Graphics Press, 2006.

———. *The Cognitive Style of PowerPoint*. 2nd ed. Cheshire, CT: Graphics Press, 2006.

van Leeuwen, Theo. "Looking Good: Aesthetics, Multimodality, and Literacy Studies." In Jennifer Rowsell and Kate Pahl, eds. *The Routledge Handbook of Literacy Studies*, pp. 426–39. New York: Routledge, 2015.

———. "New Forms of Writing, New Visual Competencies." *Visual Studies* 23, no. 2 (2008): 130–35.

van Merriënboer, Jeroen, and John Sweller. "Cognitive Load Theory in Health Professional Education: Design Principles and Strategies." *Medical Education* 44, no. 1 (2010): 85–93.

Vekiri, Ioanna. "What Is the Value of Graphical Displays in Learning?" *Educational Psychology Review* 14, no. 3 (2002): 261–312.

Ware, Colin. *Visual Thinking: For Design*. Burlington, MA: Morgan Kaufmann, 2010.

Wecker, Christof. "Slide Presentations As Speech Suppressors: When and Why Learners Miss Oral Information." *Computers & Education* 59, no. 2 (2012): 260–73.

Wilde, Judith, and Richard Wilde. *Visual Literacy: A Conceptual Approach to Graphic Problem Solving*. New York: Watson-Guptill Publications, 1991.

Williams, Robin. *The Non-Designer's Design Book: Design and Typographic Principles for the Novice*. 4th ed. San Francisco: Peachpit Press, 2015.

———. *The Non-Designer's Presentation Book: Principles for Effective Presentation Design*. San Francisco: Peachpit Press, 2009.

Yang, Fang-Ying, et al. "Tracking Learners' Visual Attention During a Multimedia Presentation in a Real Classroom." *Computers & Education* 62 (2013): 208–20.

Yates, JoAnne, and Wanda Orlikowski. "The PowerPoint Presentation and Its Corollaries: How Genres Shape Communicative Action in Organizations." In Mark Zachry and Charlotte Thralls, eds. *The Cultural Turn: Communicative Practices in Workplaces and the Professions*, pp. 67–91. Amityville, NY: Baywood Publishing, 2007.

Zull, James E. "Key Aspects of How the Brain Learns." *New Directions for Adult and Continuing Education* 110 (2006): 3–9.

Figure and Source Credits

The majority of slide originals included in this book are inspired by ineffective designs, while using subject matter derived from Wikipedia and other publicly available information. In other cases, I took instructors' good slides and did some bad things to them in order to illustrate design concepts.

Lesson 1

1.1: Background image is the Norse god Týr; in the public domain, shared via Wikimedia Commons. **1.1** and **1.2:** Information from https://en.wikipedia.org/wiki/Prologue_(Prose_Edda). Accessed May 4, 2016.
1.3 and **1.4:** Information from https://en.wikipedia.org/wiki/Buffer_strip. Accessed April 30, 2016. **1.4:** Image of buffer strips from US Department of Agriculture, Natural Resources Conservation Service, public domain, shared via Wikimedia Commons. **1.5** and **1.6:** Table screenshot and information from Juan José Eyherabide, María Inés Leaden, and Sara Alonso, "Yellow and Purple Nutsedges Survey in the Southeastern Buenos Aires Province, Argentina," *Pesquisa Agropecuária Brasileira* 36, no. 1 (2001): 205–9. Picture of yellow nutsedge shared by Blahedo under a Creative Commons Attribution–ShareAlike 2.5 Generic license via Wikimedia Commons.

Lesson 3

3.1: Image of six kingdoms of life, public domain, via Wikimedia Commons. **3.3:** Sperm whale silhouette by Rones via openclipart.org.

Information inspired by *Atlantic* article by Derek Thompson, "The Spectacular Rise and Fall of U.S. Whaling: An Innovation Story." http://www.theatlantic.com/business/archive/2012/02/the-spectacular-rise-and-fall-of-us-whaling-an-innovation-story/253355/.

Lesson 5

5.1: Step 4B: Inspired by a slide deck designed by Kevin Standish, used with permission. **5.3:** Content for slides inspired by a talk on the mimetic aspects of film by Professor Bong Eliab, used with permission. **5.8:** Neuron image by NickGorton via Wikimedia Commons under the Creative Commons Attribution–ShareAlike 3.0 Unported license. **5.9:** Catkin photograph by BlueCanoe via Wikimedia Commons under the Creative Commons Attribution–ShareAlike 3.0 Unported license.

Lesson 6

6.2: Constructed from slides in a talk on oral rehydration therapy by Tina Slusher, MD, and used with permission. **6.4:** Jellyfish image by AriellaJay via morguefile.com. **6.5** and **6.6:** These slides feature one of my favorite quotes by Catherine Adams, "PowerPoint's Pedagogy," *Phenomenology & Practice* 2, no. 1 (2008): 63–79.

Lesson 7

7.1 and **7.2:** Data was found in A. Barry, "Commerce Transactions in American Shopping Malls," *Journal of Mass Consumption* 13 (2001): 160–64. **7.3**: Information was inspired by an amalgam of ideas from several slide presentations on early Christianity and Judaism, and this Wikipedia page on the apostle Paul: https://en.wikipedia.org/wiki/Paul_the_Apostle. Accessed April 10, 2016. **7.4**, **7.5**, and **7.6:** Near and far sides of the moon courtesy of NASA, public domain. **7.7:** Satellite view of Krakatoa Islands courtesy of NASA, public domain. **7.9:** Image of Tollund Man by Sven Rosborn, public domain. **7.10:** Slide features a graphic altered from clip art found in the Microsoft Office ClipArt Gallery. Accessed December 2012.

Lesson 8

8.2: Elephant picture from Godot13 via Creative Commons Attribution-Share Alike 3.0 Unported license. **8.3:** Computer memory image, public domain, by László Szalai ("Beyond Silence") via Wikimedia Commons. **8.4:** No-headed man image is courtesy ManicMorFF via morguefile.com. **8.5:** String-on-finger image by jarhipmom via openclipart.com. **8.6:** Parts of the brain graphic by National Cancer Institute, vectorized by Jkwchui under the Creative Commons Attribution–ShareAlike 3.0 Unported license. **8.7** and **8.8:** Serial recall graph by Obli via Creative Commons

Attribution–ShareAlike 3.0 License. **8.9:** The photo of Dr. Konrad Lorenz was shared by Eurobas under a Creative Commons ShareAlike license. **8.10:** The photo of Dr. Lorenz followed by ducks is of unknown authorship, according to the terms on this page: http://psychology.wikia.com/wiki /File:Lorenz.gif. Accessed April 10, 2016.

Lesson 9

9.3: All graphics are from the oft-missed resource formerly known as the Microsoft Office ClipArt Gallery. **9.4:** Adult female bedbug by Jacopo Werther, licensed under the Creative Commons Attribution–ShareAlike 2.0 Generic license. Slide design by Tina Slusher, MD, used with permission. **9.5:** Project management ecosystem graphic from Tito Sierra under the Creative Commons 4.0 Attribution license. **9.6:** Created with data from Shrimali Ronak Baghubhai, Vijay Kumar Gupta, and Ganga Sahay Meena, "Process Optimization for the Manufacture of Kheer Mohan Employing Response Surface Methodology," *Indian Journal of Dairy Science* 68 (2015): 6. https://www.researchgate.net/publication/288828349 _Process_optimization_for_the_manufacture_of_Kheer_Mohan _employing_Response_Surface_Methodology. Accessed April 10, 2016. **9.7:** This slide includes a public domain photo of Luzenac talc and a photo of the Herkimer diamond shared by Archaeodontosaurus under the Creative Commons Attribution–ShareAlike 3.0 Unported license, with information obtained from Swapna Mukherjee, "Applied Mineralogy: Applications in Industry and Environment," *Springer Science & Business Media* (2012). **9.11:** This slide includes artwork vectorized from a screenshot of an educational video produced by Osmosis Pathophysiology, https://www.youtube.com/watch?v=oH5JmIyeoUY. Shared under the Creative Commons CC-BY-SA 4.0 international license. **9.13:** The biomes graphic includes these photos: tundra by Famartin and shared under the Creative Commons Attribution–ShareAlike 3.0 Unported license; temperate rainforest by Albh and shared under the Creative Commons Attribution–ShareAlike 3.0 Unported license; tropical rainforest by Sofiya Muntyan and shared under the Creative Commons Attribution 2.0 Generic license; desert by Rosa Cabecinhas and Alcino Cunha and shared under the Creative Commons Attribution–ShareAlike 2.0 Generic license; taiga by Igorevič and shared under the Creative Commons Attribution–ShareAlike 3.0 Unported license; grasslands by Alanscottwalker and shared under the Creative Commons Attribution–ShareAlike 3.0 Unported license.; and deciduous by Wedmann and shared under the Creative Commons Attribution–ShareAlike 3.0 Unported license. All accessed May 15, 2016. **9.14:** List of feminisms is inspired by the list on Wikipedia in the Feminism portal.

Lesson 10

10.1 and **10.6:** Constructed from slides created by David Haynes, PhD, and Kathryn Stinebaugh using the raster dataset, Global Land Cover 2000, and ArcGIS, used with permission. **10.2**, **10.8**, and **10.9:** Constructed from information from https://en.wikipedia.org/wiki/Egyptian _hieroglyphs (accessed May 13, 2016), indluding these photos: hieroglyph image by Gtoffoletto, shared under the Creative Commons Attribution–ShareAlike 4.0 International license; funeral stela image by ChrisO under the Creative Commons Attribution–ShareAlike 3.0 Unported license; and hieroglyph image by NaySay under the Creative Commons Attribution–ShareAlike 3.0 Unported license. **10.3** and **10.10:** Toothpaste tube vector art by Joost van Treeck and shared under the CC BY-SA 2.5 via Wikimedia Commons. **10.7:** This slide is by the author. It is from a talk on accessible digital communication presented in February 2016. **10.11** and **10.12:** Image is of the USS *Los Angeles*, a US Navy airship built by the Zeppelin Company. US Naval Heritage Foundation, public domain. Timeline details gathered from this Wikipedia article: https://en.wikipedia.org/wiki /Zeppelin. Accessed May 13, 2016.

Lesson 11

11.2: Herbart teaching method information is from https://en.wikipedia. org/wiki/Johann_Friedrich_Herbart. Accessed April 10, 2016.
11.3, **11.9**, and **11.11:** Constructed using "15th century ship" by Firkin via openclipart.org. **11.5:** From a slide deck on how to write effective thesis statements by Maureen Aitken, University of Minnesota Department of Writing Studies, used with permission. **11.8** and **11.10:** Screenshots come from the online color accessibility evaluation tool made available by North Carolina State University. **11.12:** Constructed using 2002 data from the Agricultural Research Service of the US Department of Agriculture, https://www.ars.usda.gov/SP2UserFiles/Place/80400525/Data/hg72 /hg72_2002.pdf. Accessed April 10, 2016.

Lesson 12

12.5: Inspired by a talk on the mimetic aspects of film by Professor Bong Eliab, used with permission. **12.6**, **12.7**, and **12.8:** Inspired by a slide deck by Nathan Roher, http://www.slideshare.net/MrRoher/communist-ussr -economysocial-class. Accessed May 16, 2016. Used with permission. **12.17:** Graphic created from the Entypo icon typeface.

Lesson 13

13.1, **13.2**, and **13.3:** Created using information from the US Department of State fact sheet "Distinctions between Human Smuggling and Human

Trafficking 2006," http://www.state.gov/documents/organization/90541
.pdf, and inspired by the graphic found at http://www.blueblindfold.gov.ie
/website/bbf/bbfweb.nsf/page/humantrafficking-traffickingsmuggling-en.
13.4 and **13.5:** Made from a slide inspired by Yoel Korenfeld Kaplan, MD,
used with permission. **13.6:** Comstock Lode lithograph, public domain,
made available by the US Library of Congress via Wikimedia Commons.
13.7: Workflow was created in LucidChart by David Haynes, PhD, and
Kathryn Stinebaugh using IPUMS-Terra, formerly TerraPop.

Lesson 14

14.1: Data derived from US Department of Agriculture Plants Database,
http://plants.usda.gov/. Accessed November 18, 2015. **14.6** and **14.7:**
Information obtained from https://en.wikipedia.org/wiki/Marcus_Garvey.
Accessed April 10, 2016. **14.9** and **14.10:** Inspired by the pros and cons
of milk consumption list at http://milk.procon.org/view.resource.php
?resourceID=656. Accessed April 10, 2016.

Lesson 15

15.1: Faces image from Dierreugia via morguefile.com. **15.2:** Graphic uses
icons by Gilad Fried (brain), Alessandro Suraci (book), Manuela Barroso
(iPad), and Piero Borgo (television), all via the Noun Project. **15.3:** Graphic
created from the Entypo icon typeface. **15.4:** Image by Matei via
morguefile.com, globe vector file from tokyoship via Creative Commons
Attribution-Share Alike 3.0 Unported license. **15.5:** Uses the open emojis
set available at emojione.com.

Lesson 16

16.1 and **16.2:** Information used to create the before and after examples
was taken from https://en.wikipedia.org/wiki/Interpersonal_relationship
but was inspired by a YouTube lecture on the same topic. **16.1:** The image
included is "Wedding Day" by Mikrash via morguefile.com.

Index

Page numbers in italics refer to figures.

accessibility
    alternative text use, 31, 37,
        38–39
    best practices of, 25–26
    color and, 111, 113–16, *115,*
        116, 120
    distributing slides and, 31
    fonts and, 124, 128, 139
    handouts and, 33–37, 189
    layouts and, 99
    screen readers (slides) and, 31,
        99, 139, 161, 164
    screen readers (handouts) and,
        33–34, 36, 37
    slide themes and, 72
    transcripts and, 181
    WordArt and, 139
    active processing theory, 19
    agenda slide, 28, *28,* 32
    all caps, 137–38, *137*
Alley, Michael, 59, 191

alternative text, 31, 37, 38–39
animation, 145–46, 147, 152–53,
    183, 191
annotation, 145, 150–51, 183, 191
    narrating, 151
assertion-evidence (A-E) structure,
    59–61, *60,* 62–65, 67, 76, *76*
asynchronous presentation, 22, 50,
    98–99, 181–82
attention, 3, 10, 18, 42, 70, 145, 183
attention guiding, 145, 191
    color and, 148–49, *149*
    progressive disclosure and,
        145–48, *148,* 153, 183
    shapes and, 149–50, *150,* 152

bold, 132–34, *132, 134*
bullet points
    alternatives to, 48–50
    economy in use of, 159–60, *160*
    handouts and, 36, 38

logic of, 156–59, *157, 159*
parallel structure in, 157–59,
    166
punctuation of, 165
shapes of, 163–65, *164, 165,*
    166
strengths of, 155–56
tool for, 160–61
weaknesses of, 3, 41–44
versus ordered list, 162–63

centered text, 134, *135*
charts and graphs, 4, 60
citations (receiving), 169, 175
citations (sources), 171, 172–73,
    190, 191
clarity, 10, 15, 26, 111, 129–30
cognitive processing, 19
coherence principle, 69–70
cohesion, 3, 10, 15, 83–84, 94, 110,
    124–25
color
    accessibility and, 111, 113–16,
        115, 116, 120
    attention guiding and, 148–49,
        149
    color-coding, 111
    systems, 3, 110–12, 120–21,
        190
    communication and, 107–10,
        109, 110, 112, 116–17
    contrast and, 112, *113,* 120, 189
    gradients, 118, *119*
    hexadecimal values, 114, 119,
        120
    palettes, predefined, 119
    RGB values, 114, 119, 120
    vibrations between, 118, *118*
complex structures, 151–52,
    152, 189,
composition, 93–96, 101, 104–5

conceal and reveal. *See* progressive
    disclosure
concept maps, 50
conference presentation, 175
consistency, 3, 10, 15, 94, 97,
    173, 190
    graphics and, 83–84, *83, 84,*
        190,
    fonts and, 3, 123–24, 190
contact information, 167, 168–69,
    170, 172, 176, 191
copyright, 173
Craft of Scientific Presentations
    (Alley), 59, 191
Creative Commons, 168, 169, 174,
    176, 177, 191
cultural specificity, 88, 94, 102,
    103, 164
customized layout, 104

dates, 168, 169
decluttering, 51, 57–58
decorative graphics, 69–70, 72–75,
    73–75, 78
digital citizenry, 167, 191
display font, 126, *126,* 142
dual channel theory, 19
Duarte, Nancy, 191

effective comparison, 62, *63*
end matter slide, 169–72
essential message, 46, 51, 59, 61,
    99–100,

finishing medium, 183
first slide, 167–68, *168*
fonts
    accessibility and, 124, 128, 139
    bold, 132–34, *132, 134*
    comparison of, 142
    compatibility of, 127

consistency of, 3, 123–24, 190

contrasts between, 130–31, *131*

display, 126, *126*, 142

emphasis in, 124–25, 128, 132–34

families, 124–25, *125*, 127–28

italics, 129

plain, 125–27, *126*, 142

sans-serif, 127–28, 142

serif, 127–28, 142

size for line spacing, 141

weight, 125, *125*

formatting. *See* text formatting

full-justified text, 135–36, *136*

full-screen image with title, 50, *50*, 55, *56*

Gestalt principles, 89–91, *90, 91*, 92

graphic design, 2, 10, 51, 78, 83–84, 104–5, 191

graphic organizer slide, 26–27, *27*

graphics, 46–48,
    assertion-evidence (A-E) structure and, 59–60

    charts and graphs, 4, 60

    concept maps, 50

    consistency of, 83–84, *83, 84*, 190

    decorative, 69–70, 72–75, *73–75*, 78

    evocative, 64–65, *65*

    finding images and, 173–174

    full-screen image with title, 50, *50*, 55, *56*

    illuminative, 75–78, *75, 77*

    infographics, 50

    labels and, 49, *49*, 66, *66*, 190

    line art as, 174

    logos, 71, 168, 169, 175

    motivational, 167, 168, 171

    planning use of, 182–83

    royalties and, 173

    selection of, 3–4, 65, 69, 72–79, 190

    stock photos, 70, *74*, 168

    timeline, 103–4, *103*, 151

guidepost slide, 4, 29–30, *30*, 32, 180, 183–84, 189

handouts, 179–80, 182, 186, 189

    accessibility and, 33–37, 189

    as alternative to slide text, 4

    from text-only outline of slide deck, 38–39

    recommended resources information and, 171

    section headings in, 36, 38

    separate from slide content, 33–35

    universal design and, 35

    white space and, 36

hexadecimal values, 114, 119, 120

hiding slides, 184

hyperlinks, 37, 38, 136–37

illuminative graphics, 75–78, *75, 77*

images. *See* graphics

indents and tabs. *See* text formatting

infographics, 50

information value, 101, *101*

intentionality, 3, 15, 22, 46, 76, 112

interacting with visuals, 156

italics. *See* text formatting

iteration, 183, 184

justification, text. *See* text formatting

kinesthetic learning, 44
knowledge retention, 59, 183

last slide, 171–72, *172*
layouts, 93–94
    customized, 104
    predefined, 31, 96–99, *96*, 190
    Z-pattern, 97–98, *97*, 146
learning objective slide, 28–29, *29*
lecture, 19–20, 179–80, 186, 191
    script writing, 2, 179–82, 183
left-justified text, 134, *135*
left-to-right organization, 102–4,
    102, *103*, 146
letting go, 184–85
limited capacity theory, 19
line art, 174
line spacing. *See* text formatting
lines, 84–87, *85*, *86*, *87*, *103*
lists
    ordered, 36, 38, 162–63, 166
    versus bullet points, 162–63
lists tool (word processing), 36, 38
logos, 71, 168, 169, 175

Malamed, Connie, 192
Mayer, Richard, 19
media credits, 170, *170*, 190, 191
metadata, 176–77, 191
motivational graphics. *See* graphics
multimedia learning 1, 19, 66,
    69–70, 82

negative space. *See* white space
Non-designer's Design Book, The
    (Williams), 130, 191
note taking, 44

organizational support slides, 4
outline slide, *42*

paragraph styles (word processors),
    36, 38
parallel structure, 157–59, 166
plain font, 125–27, *126*, 142
predefined layout, 31, 96–99, *96*,
    190
Presentation Zen (Reynolds), 55
prettyness, 3, 9–11
preview slide, 4, 26–29, 180,
    183–84, 189
Prezi, 151–52
principles of academic slide design,
    2–5, 189–91
progressive disclosure, 145–48,
    148, 153, 183
proximity (Gestalt principle),
    89–91, *90*

recap slide, 30, 189
recommended resources, 171, *171*
redundancy principle, 20, 22, 23
rehearsing, 182, 184
repetition, 25, 26, 30
retention, 59, 183
Reynolds, Garr, 55
RGB values, 114, 119, 120

sans-serif font, 127–28, 142
scannability, 36, 138, 139, 161–62,
screen readers (slides). *See*
    accessibility
screen readers (handouts).
    See accessibility
script writing, 2, 179–82, 183
sentence case, 137–38, *138*
serif font, 127–28, 142
shapes, 87–88, *87*, *88*,
    attention guiding and, 149–50,
    150, 152
    of bullet points, 163–65, *164*,
    165, 166

your online bookshop

**Thank you for your Wordery
order. We hope you enjoy your
book #HappyReading**

your online bookshop

20170719280801

contrast between, 88–89, 189
emotions and, 88, *89*
similarity (Gestalt principle), 89,
    91, *91*
Slide Master, 96, 98, 101, 104, 164
slide types
    agenda, 28, *28*, 32
    end matter, 169–72
    first, 167–68, *168*
    guidepost, 4, 29–30, *30*, 32,
        180, 183–84, 189
    graphic organizer, 26–27, *27*
    last, 171–72, *172*
    learning objective, 28–29, *29*
    organizational support, 4
    outline, *42*
    preview, 4, 26–29, 180,
        183–84, 189
    recap, 30, 189
slidedoc, 22, 23
Slide:ology (Duarte), 191
sliderding, 22, 23
slides
    creation criteria for, 20–21
    deck-to-outline conversion of,
        38
    distributing, 31
    hiding, 184
    interacting with, 156
    purpose of, 67
    numbering and, 30–31, 32, 190
    sharing of, 176
    talking through, 88
    themes in design of, 71–72, *71*
    titles and, 31
    topic-subtopic structure of, *11*,
        17–19, *65*, 101
    transitions and, 146
    unimodal design of, 22, 23
    use as handouts, 18, 23,
        33–34, *34*

use as teleprompter, 18, 23, 41,
    45–46, *45*, 181
slidewire, 22, 23
SmartArt, 82, *83*
spatial contiguity principle, 66
source information. *See* citations
    (sources)
stock photos, 70, *74*, 168
storyboarding, 180, 182–83
student-centered design, 133–34
student engagement, 179
squint test, 92

tables, 36, 38
talking through slides, 88
talking through annotations, 151
testing, 19, 184
text-based treatment, 49, *49*
text formatting
    all caps, 137–38, *137*
    bold, 132–34, *132*, *134*
    indents and tabs, 165–66
    italics, 129
    justification, center, 134, *135*
    justification, full, 135–36, *136*
    justification, left, 134, *135*
    line spacing, 139–42, *140*,
        141, 143
    paragraph styles (word
        processors), 36, 38
    sentence case, 137–38, *138*
    title case, 137–38
    underlining, 128
timeline, 103–4, *103*, 151
title case, 137–38
topic-subtopic structure, *11*,
    17–19, *65*, 101
transcripts, 181
Twitter, 175
typeface. *See* fonts

typography, 123. *See also* fonts
    transparent, 123, 127, 129, 136

underlined text, 128
unimodal slide design, 22, 23
universal design, 25–26
URL shortener, 136–37, *137*, 186

Venn diagram, 147–48, *147, 148*
verbal-visual integration, 20
visual communication, 15, 46,
    47, 191
Visual Design Solutions (Malamed),
    192
visual hierarchy, 94, 99–100,
    104–5, 190

visual journal, 16, 58, 92
visual literacy, 16, 69, 82, 88,
    141, 191
visual metaphor, *28, 43, 151*
visual system, 190
visuospatial communication, 28,
    29–30, 43, 81–82, 103–4

white space, 4, 53–55, *54, 55*,
    139–41, 161–62, 190
    for emphasis, 56, *57*, 58
Williams, Robin, 130, 191
WordArt, 138–39, *139*
wordiness, 3, 18, 33, 44–46, *57, 146*

Z-pattern, 97–98, *97*, 146

Acknowledgments

Academic Adviser: Angelica Pazurek *Audio Production:* Seward Sound
Catering: Sage Spoon Living *Cheerleading:* Mahsa Abassi, Ilene Alexander,
Nesrin Bakir, Kalli Ann Binkowski, Marina Bluvstein, Ben Chase,
Chen Chen, KT Cragg, Heather Dorr, Jennifer Englund, Jane Fandrey,
Karen Fandrey, Lora Fandrey, Sonny Fandrey, Jeannette George,
Sophia Gladding, Brett Hendel-Paterson, Anne Hunt, Tom Kell,
Jolie Kennedy, Scott Krenz, Deborah Levison, Amy LimBybliw,
Deb Ludowese, Debra Luedtke, Lauren Marsh, Scott Marshall,
Otto Marquardt, Adam Mayfield, Charlie Mayfield, Fritz Mayfield,
Harry Mayfield, Annette McNamara, Stephanie Midler, Rebecca Moss,
Joan Portel, Sara Schoen, Mark Schoenbaum, Peg Sherven, Emily Stull
Richardson, Lee Thomas, Susan Tade, Kim Wilcox, Daniel Woldeab
Consultation: Lynell Burmark, Julie Dirksen *Content Review:*
Ira Cummings, Joel Dickinson, Karen Fandrey, Geri Huigbretse,
Jolie Kennedy, Amy LimBybliw, Alison Link, Annette McNamara,
Tonu Mikk, Amy Neeser, Constance Pepin *Copyediting:* Amy LimBybliw,
Cristina Lopez *Indexing:* Jon Jeffryes *Manuscript Critique:* Maureen Aitken,
Michael Alley, Brad Hokanson, Rachel Stassen-Berger

And one more word: Protected time to write and illustrate this book
would not have been possible without steadfast and loving support
from Ben and the many hours of time together sacrificed by Mom and Dad,
Jane and Lora, and their families. My deepest and most especial thanks
to each of you.

Invite Ann

to lead a workshop at your school, speak at your department meeting, or consult with you on your next conference presentation, job talk, or high-profile lecture. Contact her at **academicslidedesign.org**.

CPSIA information can be obtained
at www.ICGtesting.com
Printed in the USA
LVOW05s0110180717
541567LV00013B/14/P